DIMENSIONS of Faith

Okey Onuzo, M.D.

To my wife Mariam and my children Dilichi, Chinaza Dinachi and Chibundu, with whom I have been in this walk of faith together.

All Bible quotations are from the King James version except where otherwise indicated.

FIRST EDITION

All rights reserved including the right of reproduction in any form except with the author's written permission.

Copyright © Dr. Okey Onuzo 1990

Published by: Life Link Worldwide, Inc., 350 Marley Drive, College Park, Ga. 30349, Tel. (1) (404) 994-1683

ISBN 1-880608-01-4

Worldwide Distribution

NIGERIA - Life Publications, 1, Oba Docemo Street, G.R.A. Ikeja, Lagos, NIGERIA.

UNITED KINGDOM - Providence Books, 296 Wilbraham Road, Charlton cum Hardy, Manchester M21 1UG, Tel. (44) (061) 881-5771

Printed in the United States of America

CONTENTS

Foreword	*v*
Preface	*vii*
Acknowledgement	*ix*
1. What is Faith?	11
2. The Guarantor and His Guaranties	15
The Guarantor's Guaranties	22
3. The Natural Faith	26
4. The Spiritual and the Natural in Faith	33
5. The Saving Faith	38
How to Receive the Saving Grace through Faith	47
6. The Universal and the Particular in Faith	50
7. The Three Stages of a Christian's Walk of Faith	56
8. The Honeymoon Faith	60
9. The School of Faith	64
10. Integrating the Lessons of the school of Faith	81
The Secret of Spiritual Strength	81
The Fruit of the Holy Spirit and the	
Spiritual Strength of the Disciples	84
Abraham	87
King Saul	89
King David	94
Summary of the School of Faith	99
11. Faith as a Seed	101
12. Fulfillingour obedience of Christ	105

13. Ingredients of Creative Faith	111
Believing	113
Confessing and Expecting the Object of our Faith	115
Receiving the Object of our Faith	117
Creative Faith and the Spoken Word	117
14. Patience	121
15. Praise and Thanksgiving	125
16. The Seed must Die	129
17. Faith beyond the Grave	138
18. Conversational Prayer	144
19. The Dimensions of Faith	147

Foreword

You will never learn how faith works in its varied dimensions as outlined in this book until your life depends on it.

I learnt faith in a very practical way soon after I entered Bible College in 1962. I had to trust God for fees and pocket money.

The first shock came when I could not muster enough faith just for a postage stamp. I prayed daily for nearly two weeks before I got the stamp. Then I needed one pound. That took three weeks of hard praying. I shuddered at the thought of how many weeks of agonizing prayer it would take to have faith for fifty pounds.

One day, I asked the Lord why faith for miracles was so hard to come by. I soon learnt that one cannot programme God like a computer, or make Him do what you like by following some formulae. The Lord helped me to understand that faith that moves mountains is a matter of the nature and depth of one's personal relationship with Him, the God of miracles.

Every Christian is born to win, but we know that it is not automatic. Faith is the key that unlocks many doors to a life of victory and power.

In this book, rightly titled *Dimensions of Faith*, my good friend Dr. Okey Onuzo has brought together many aspects of faith. Each one has been tested in the furnace of his own experience with the Lord. He not only writes about faith, but lives by faith.

I commend this book to the entire body of Christ universal, and to God our Lord, the Father of our Lord Jesus Christ who taught us in His word that, *"The Just shall live by Faith"*, Amen.

Paul Jinadu

Preface

Faith explosion may be an appropriate description of the last fifty years of Church History Worldwide. Suddenly faith and the benefits the believer derives by walking according to its principles took the front seat in evangelical teaching and preaching giving rise to many Global Ministries that have touched several millions of lives. Large Ministries with tele-evangelistic arms all over the World, bear eloquent testimony to the fact that indeed, faith in God, and in His Son Jesus Christ as revealed in His Holy Book the Bible can break new frontiers, and that *with God nothing is impossible.* The understanding of the basis and implications of Bible Faith has changed, and is still changing the lives of men and women across the globe for the better.

But in spite of these monumental efforts and results, Saint Paul's declaration in his second letter to the Thessalonians, to the effect that not all men have faith, is still very much true today as when it was written nearly two thousand years ago.

There are those who still argue that Bible faith is not logically defensible, and so cannot really be intellectually articulated. Even some in the worldwide Christian family can still be heard to say that what we need to do is simply believe it. We do not really have to think about it.

Experience however tells us clearly that our faith, if it is to be meaningful and useful to us, must be so well developed and articulated that it can handle our personal conflicts and questions as diverse as they may be, with respect to the

Almighty God, and the realities of life and living. It must be able to answer our doubts and reservations about these and similar questions like, sin, forgiveness, the new birth, eternal judgement, prosperity, fortunes and the misfortunes of life, as well as human suffering and the lack of it. It must above all provide us with the armour to battle the vicissitudes or the ups and downs of life, enabling us to convert each obstacle into a stepping stone.

It is imperative therefore that we must know what faith is, how it operates, and the various dimensions of it so as to help us experience victory in every circumstance that we are confronted with.

To be able to convert each obstacle into a stepping stone is a wonderful testimony that should be the joyful experience of every believer, and a fishing tool in the hands of every witness and disciple for the expansion of the kingdom of God. My prayer is that the Holy Spirit will use what is shared here to bring many sons and daughters of the kingdom to glory, in Jesus name, AMEN.

Dr. Okey Onuzo
21st. January, 1990

Acknowledgement

I thank the Lord very much for enabling me to write this book. In a sense it has been very long in coming, and this is as it should be when dealing with a subject of this nature.

I must thank Rev. Paul Jinadu for accepting to write the foreword to this book. I recall a great deal of the sermons he preached in Ibadan in the seventies, some in the university where I was a student, and some in his church which I attended now and again. Many of them are still so fresh in my memory, and constitute the base of some of my own sermons today.

I am indebted to Miss Anne Rotimi Ndego for carefully going through this manuscript and making very relevant changes, some of which led to complete text restructuring, and to Toyin and Femi Ogundipe for their usual final touches.

My wife and I lived through a great deal of these dimensions together, and without her support I may have buckled under some of the pressures of the time.

I have discovered that God sharpens our understanding of a thought by bringing someone to share their burdens with us. We may have experienced some dimensions of faith ourselves, but sharing them with someone else goes a long way to synthesize and clarify them to us, giving us a more rewarding insight. I must therefore thank all those who have come my way as a counsellor, and have been encouraged to share with me very intimately. Quite unknown to them, they have in a very large measure contributed to the insights that have been shared here.

Finally, it is my prayer that all those who benefit from what is shared herein, will return all praise and glory to God our Father, who loved us so much that He sent us His Son Jesus to die for us thereby creating the firm basis for faith in God. To Him alone be glory forever, AMEN.

Chapter 1

WHAT IS FAITH?

The eleventh chapter of the book of Hebrews tells us rather clearly that *"Faith is the substance of things hoped for, the evidence of things not seen."*

Accepting that we need further help with that, the more modern translations went ahead to proffer: *"To have faith is to be sure of the things we hope for, to be certain of the things we cannot see."* [Good News Bible] The Revised Standard Version puts it this way: *"Now faith is the assurance of things hoped for, the conviction of things not seen."*

At the end of the day, what we come away with is that the task before us with respect to faith is how to impart certainty to things in the future that are normally uncertain. *"How can you be sure?"* is the bottom line question. To simply repeat, *"Oh I am definitely sure about it,"* is only re-affirming what one had said earlier, and even in that, there is a certain element of doubt. It has not in any way imparted the much desired certainty.

Another person may simply reply with deep candour: *"Oh I believe it with all my heart."* Indeed you may, but that in no way confers certainty to something that is basically uncertain.

In a sense faith has a great deal to do with guaranties. In business today, there are certain instruments of transaction that are guaranteed. There are some businessmen and women, as well as some stores that will take nothing but cash in a transaction, for several reasons. Others accept cash or bank cheques only, while others go as far as accepting personal cheques. A bank cheque is guaranteed by the resources of an institution, and so has a higher degree of credibility when compared to a personal cheque which hangs on the integrity of the individual issuing it. As a result of this, some business men will accept a bank cheque, but never a personal cheque. The guarantee behind a bank cheque is sufficient basis to release their goods to their customer, with the confidence that the bank will transfer the money to their accounts in due course.

By the same token, an ordinary cheque from a business organisation has more credibility than an ordinary cheque from an individual. The argument is that a business organisation provides a higher level of guarantee of eventual payment than an individual.

From these analogies, it is obvious that faith does not consist of mere affirmations. It has a great deal to do with back up guarantees. In other words, one does not really develop faith by merely saying, *"Oh I do honestly believe,"* particularly where the guarantees behind that article of faith has not even been examined at all.

When the Bible declares that *"Faith is the substance of things hoped for, the evidence of things not seen,"* it is referring to these guarantees that ensure for the individual that his or her faith object will materialize no matter the obstacles that are lined up against him or her. For an individual to have this kind of faith being spoken of here, the implication is that he or she knows the *Guarantor* of the faith, and the terms and conditions of His *Guaranties.*

This is because the certainty of eventual redemption or materialization rests solely on the integrity and ability of the *Guarantor,* and the terms and conditions of His *Guaranties.*

To claim to have faith without knowing either the guarantor or the terms and conditions of His guarantee, is to have what we may describe as *A baseless faith,* or in our local parlance, *"superficial believism."* which is actually another name for wishful thinking, because it has no solid base.

Indeed, *"Faith is the substance of things hoped for, the evidence of things not seen,"* but only to those who appreciate the basis of it, and so understand its dynamics, which implies the laws that govern it, or its terms and conditions.

But there are those who may argue that if you can articulate faith in such finite terms, then it ceases to be faith. The impression they have of faith is, *something you do not have to understand, which you have to believe anyway.*

Sometime ago, one gentleman and his wife told me that to imply that faith can be understood is a gross mis-representation. There still will be lots and lots of questions that one will need answered for which there are no convincing answers. All you need to do is believe it if you like, reject it if you don't, but never question it.

That kind of position amounts to no more than intellectual slavery. The implication is that faith is not rational.

When we examine the issue thoroughly, we find that faith as taught by the Bible requires you to make just one, and only one seemingly blind assumption. That assumption has to do with the *Source Of Faith.* This is the way the Bible puts it.

"But without faith it is impossible to please him; For he that cometh to God *must believe that He is,* and that he is a rewarder of them that diligently seek him [Hebrews 11:6 KJV]

He that comes to God must believe that God exists. This is the *ab-initio* or the initial presumption that the Bible calls for. It is the demand of the One the Bible describes as the *Almighty God,* the *Pre-eminent One.* The implication is that except you make this presumption, you will not be able to experience the fact that God is a rewarder of those who diligently seek Him. That in itself implies personalization, which individualizes the relationship between a person and his or her God. The individual will be in a position to make a personal discovery: That God is a rewarder of those who diligently seek Him.

To seek to take a step farther back than that position, is not to have a source of faith. But when you accept the fact of the reality of God, then you will be in a position to make meaning out of the diversities in life. God will then become to you the *Guarantor* of faith, and through a thorough study of the Bible you will become familiar with the terms and conditions of His *Guaranties.* Those who are unwilling to make this all important presumption, never discover a personal God, and His mighty hand that is heavily laden with rewards.

As we examine the dimensions of faith, we shall concentrate on the *Guarantor* and His *Guaranties,* in order to be able to get a huge chunk of His rewards.

Chapter 2

THE GUARANTOR AND HIS GUARANTIES

"Then Moses said to God, Indeed when I come to the children of Israel and say to them, the God of your fathers have sent me to you, and they say to me, what is His name? what shall I say to them?"

"And God said to Moses, '*I AM WHO I AM.*' *Thus you shall say to the children of Israel, I AM has sent me to you.*" [Exodus 3:13,14 NKJ]

When Moses was confronted by this problem of identification, after his own personal encounter with God, it would appear that the initial reply that God gave him left him as baffled as before. *"I AM WHO I AM."* The natural question that follows then will be; "who are you, I still do not know you. The reply has not helped me."

It would appear that God was well aware of Moses' dilemma, and so in the next verse He gave him a reference standard.

> "Moreover, God said to Moses, thus you shall say to the children of Israel: The Lord God of your fathers, the God of Abraham, the God of Isaac, and the God of Jacob, has sent me to you. This is my name forever, and this is My memorial to all generations." [Exodus 3:15 NKJ]

The children of Israel were in a position to appreciate that reference. Their fathers had told them of the Almighty God of their ancestors, Abraham, Isaac and Jacob. Although they were not there, they had vivid stories that helped them to visualize what could easily happen to them if that God were to return to their help the way He helped their great grandfathers.

By providing a reference they could relate with, God was providing some anchor on which faith could rest. Some foundation if you please, on which faith could start in order for it to begin to grow. Something like: "going from the known to the unknown." The God of Abraham, Isaac and Jacob, is a recognisable God who had attributes that could be appreciated by the people. The experience was indirect. They had no reason to believe that their ancestors did not know what they were talking about when they spoke gloriously of their experiences with the God who was personal to them.

The God of Abraham, Isaac and Jacob, was a God who made promises and kept them; who demanded obedience and blessed those who obeyed; who honoured faith and rewarded it handsomely. He was a God who intervened on the behalf of those who worshipped Him.

By telling Moses to tell the people that *I AM* had sent him; I AM, the God of Abraham, Isaac and Jacob, God was implying that those His attributes recognisable in His relationship with their great grandparents, had not changed. In other words, *I AM* still everything you had been told I was. I have not changed. Based on what you had been told about me, which was authenticated or proved right in the experiences of those who walked with me, you in your generation can begin to develop your own experience, that is, your own personal experience of me, and should expect me to be consistent with my nature which I demonstrated in the experiences of Abraham, Isaac and Jacob.

What we are faced with here is the problem of trying to make Someone we cannot see or touch, real, so that our minds can begin to appreciate Him. Put differently, we must adduce finiteness to someone who is essentially *Infinite*, in order to give our rational minds an acceptable orientation. This is what will become the rudiments or basis of what we may call an intellectually defensible faith or a faith that one can logically defend.

But then, someone may say: not having the priviledge of being a direct descendant of Abraham poses a basic problem. The apostle Paul, a man who had the wonderful priviledge of articulating a well developed intellectual faith, with very deep spiritual roots, answered that question in his letter to the Romans.

> "But God shows His anger from heaven against all sinful, evil men who push away the truth from them. For the truth about God is known to them instinctively; God has put this knowledge in their hearts. Since earliest times men have seen the earth and sky and all God made, and have known of his existence and great eternal power. So they will have no excuse (when they stand before God at Judgement day).
>
> Yes, they knew about Him all right, but they wouldn't admit it or worship Him for all His daily care. And after a while they began to think up silly ideas of what God was like and what He wanted them to do. The result was that their foolish minds became dark and confused. Claiming themselves to be wise without God, they became utter fools instead. And then, instead of worshipping the glorious, ever-living God, they took wood and stone and made idols for themselves, carving them to look like mere birds and animals and snakes and puny men." [Romans 1:18-23 LB]

The contention of the apostle is that although one may not have the priviledge of an authenticated genealogical experience of a personal God, the knowledge of the reality of God can be found in two key areas: the soul of man the harbinger of his instincts, and nature. In an earlier work, *From Everlasting To Everlasting*, we showed that the conscience of man, resident in his soul, is the reservoir of the true knowledge of God in the heart of man, after the fall of man.

Some advocates of idolatry contend that an idol is simply a symbol, designed to represent the God they cannot impart tangibility to otherwise. If that is all there is to it, then we would conclude that their error is simply a developmental stage in spiritual awareness. But anybody who is accustomed to the ways of seasoned idolaters and their blood cuddling orgies, will readily understand that idolatry is only one form of spiritism, where God is actually replaced by Lucifer and his demons. The apostle Paul was quick to point this out when he said:

> "What I am saying is that those who offer food to these idols are united together in sacrificing to demons, certainly not to God. And I don't want any of you to be partners with demons when you eat the same food, along with the heathen, that has been offered to these idols. You cannot drink from the cup at the Lord's Table and at Satan's table too. You cannot eat bread both at the Lord's Table and at Satan's table." [1st Corinthians 10 : 19-21 LB]

Knowing God from instinct and nature like the Bible said in the Book of Romans Chapter 1, is knowledge that we are supposed to derive from within and from without us. From within, by sensing in us the void left by the departure of the Spirit of God at the fall of man, thereby rendering our human spirit non-functional, and identifying that yearning within every man to reach out beyond himself to someone greater, through whom he can achieve a deeper and wider expression of himself. From without by appreciating the depth, sophistication or complexity of creation and thereby appreciating the immensity of the God who brought it all into existence. The apostle was contending that those who do not have the priviledge and opportunity of historical and genealogical relationship with Abraham can still develop their own independent base on which faith can sprout.

All these have to do with an appreciation of the *Guarantor* of faith, in order that a baseline for the development of faith can be established.

The *Guarantor* of faith incidentally, is also the *Source of faith. He is the Ultimate, the Beginning and the End.* Before Him and beyond Him stands nothing. This was the thought the apostle was echoing to the Hebrews in his letter about the oath with which the Almighty God guaranteed the new covenant in Christ. Since there was nothing beyond God, nor before Him, nothing greater than He, He could swear by no other than by Himself.

> "For instance, there was God's promise to Abraham: *GOD took an oath in his own name, since there was no one greater to swear by,* that He would bless Abraham again and again, and give him a son and make him the father of a great nation of people. Then Abraham waited patiently until finally God gave him a son, Isaac, just as He promised.
>
> When a man takes an oath, he is calling on someone greater than himself to force him to do what he has promised, or to punish him if he later refuses to do it; the oath ends all arguments about it. God also bound Himself with an oath, so that those he promised to help would be perfectly sure and never need to wonder whether He might change His plans." [Hebrews 6:13-17 LB].

When the Bible says that; *"Without faith it is impossible to please God,"* it is speaking about the compulsory demands of the *Guarantor* and the *Source of Faith*.

That passage is actually aimed at man's volition or the exercise of his will, and his humility before his creator. A man can arrogantly refuse to accept the reality of his creator, claiming that his intellect or mind is not persuaded. He might then proceed to offer alternative explanations for the realities that exist in life and nature. As disjointed and incomplete as these explanations may be, and often as illogical too, he may cling to them tenaciously or tightly, even against reason. This is the fall out of volition, by which I mean the result of man's ability to make choices which the Almighty God allowed him to have at creation. The Almighty is constrained or bound by the limitations which He has imposed on Himself by granting man volition at his creation, to watch as it were helplessly, thereby allowing man to think and do as he chooses; and we may note this limitation in His declared intention in the book of Genesis chapter 1, verse 26: *"And God said, Let us make man in our image, after our likeness..."*

When man exercised this free will outside God's commands in the garden of Eden, he lost the restraint hitherto imposed by the Spirit of God.

"And the Lord God said, Behold the man is become as one of us, to know good and evil:--" (In other words, his free will had become totally unlimited.) [Genesis 3:22 KJV]

But to man's repeated demands for a greater expression of His reality, He replies with the resounding: *I AM THAT I AM*. Tell them that *I AM* has sent you. They may come with that alone, and then *they will discover me*. "He that cometh to God must first believe that He is". The expression, 'must first believe that He is,' is the *ab-initio* state of mind or the initial or primary state of mind an individual must have to discover God. Anybody who comes otherwise will find the door to the revelation knowledge of God written with the bold inscription: **"CLOSED."**

The *Guarantor* and the *Source of all Faith* is accessible, but only on His own terms and conditions. It is His right to insist that all those who seek to discover Him must come convinced that He exists. He is not prepared to offer anything beyond that.

Suppose we were to entertain human pride and arrogance before the Creator for one second, and reproduce a parallel in order to aid understanding. Suppose then that we were to impart animity to inanimity or simply put, impart life to a non-living thing, and offer an object of art like a sculpture the capacity to speak. This object of art made by man then desires to know its maker. The maker which in this case is man, then says to it: "you have to accept the fact of my existence first, before you can experience practically the effect of my presence".

If the object of art really wants to understand itself, it should know that its own very existence constitutes the reason for its maker's existence. The work of art itself is the most eloquent testimony of the existence and reality of its maker, except of course it subscribes to or accepts the ridiculous contention that it is a by-product of chance. On the face of it, one can see, that the sculptor is not really asking too much of his work of art. Where the problem will exist, is if the sculpture were to return to say: *"but I still could not find my maker."*

When the Bible says that he that comes to God, and I dare to add, in order to discover Him, must first believe that He exists, it is putting forward God's minimum requirement for the revelation of Himself to man. He will do it no other way.

We may summarize what we are talking about here as the rights, the priviledges and the demands of the *Guarantor*, and the *Source of Faith*. When the Bible implies that the Almighty God is *Omnipresent, Omniscient* and *Omnipotent*, it is speaking about the rights of deity which call, not for question but for discovery. It is calling on the creatures to see how they can integrate or add together, the diversities or differences they have observed in life into these attributes of their creator. This is a progressive search, and over the years, the knowledge that has been derived from this search has influenced every facet of human life both in the Sciences and in the Arts, in Politics and Sociology, as well as in works of Art.

An indispensable part of this discovery is the terms and conditions of the *Guarantor's Guaranties*, which we shall proceed to look at now.

The Guarantor's Guaranties

In the book of Romans chapter 10 and verse 17, we read these words:

"So then faith comes by hearing, and hearing by the word of God."

The implication of this passage is quite universal in its scope and dimension. Faith comes through the understanding of the Guarantor and the terms and conditions of His guarantees. Faith comes by hearing the word of God, which is a revelation of the nature of God, His will in time and history, and the conditions He has set for a personalized relationship with Him. *"Faith, the substance of things hoped for, and the evidence of things not seen"* is by implication a by-product of knowledge, the revelation knowledge of the Almighty God.

The fact that this faith is a by-product of knowledge immediately reveals a vital limitation to its existence and thereby its effectiveness. In other words, the more you have the revelation knowledge of God, the more you have faith. In contrast, the less you have of the revelation knowledge of God the less faith you have.

First of all, *"he that cometh to God must first believe that he is."* That is *Gate Number One*. It is not enough to enter this gate, because the apostle James did caution that mere belief in the existence of God offers very little if any consolation at all.

"You believe that there is one God. You do well. Even the demons believe and tremble." [James 2:19 NKJ]

The implication is that the demons who have rebelled against God know that indeed the Almighty God exists, and the mere thought of His due judgement of their rebellion causes them to tremble. So mere belief, as good as it sounds, offers no benefits at all. It is a good beginning, but remains only a beginning.

To understand that God is a rewarder of them that diligently seek Him, implies more than mere belief. It implies knowledge of God beyond the very rudimentary. It implies a personalized experience of the interventionist roles of God on behalf of those who worship Him, a fact the prophet

Hanani captured with these words, in his indictment against King Asa:

> "For the eyes of the Lord run to and fro throughout the whole earth, to show Himself strong on behalf of those whose heart is loyal to Him..." [2nd Chronicles 16:9 NKJ]

We are accustomed to the selective *amnesia* (loss of memory) of us mortals, a fact eloquently testified to by Mark Anthony in Shakespeare's Julius Caesar where he said: *"The evil that men do, lives after them. The good is oft interred with their bones."*

But in God's interventionist role as observed by the seer Hanani, He is consistently seeking out opportunities to demonstrate to those loyal to Him, that His awesome or mighty powers are available to defend, protect and provide for them.

When the Bible therefore declares that faith comes by a deep understanding of the word of God, it is referring to this insight into the nature of God, and the conditions He has set for a personalized relationship with Him.

Indeed this is the object of this book. To explore the dimensions of this faith, in order to solidify its base and enhance its effectiveness as an instrument for reaching this outstretched arm of God, heavily laden with rewards.

To speak about the *Dimensions of Faith* therefore is to speak about an exploration of the terms and conditions of the guarantor's guaranties.

By His grace we shall speak of the dimensions we have learnt, the dimensions we have heard about, and the dimensions we have experienced. So long as God is God, this study will remain inexhaustible, until we are totally transformed into the full image of God's Son, our Lord and Saviour Jesus

Christ of whom it was reported that the work of the Holy Spirit of God in Him and through Him, was without limitations. [John 3:34]

Chapter 3

THE NATURAL FAITH

There is a sense in which the use of the word natural in connection with faith is a contradiction in terms. This is because faith is the language with which the Spirit of God communicates with the spirit of man. So if one exercises faith under normal circumstances, by implication one may be said to be spiritual to a certain degree.

We must distinguish faith as a language of the spirit from the natural faith. There is no individual who does not live by faith. In fact without faith, life as we know it today will be impossible.

Take the example of eating out at a restaurant. It calls for a great amount of faith which we have all come to take for granted. Unless there is a definite incident that has compelled us to believe otherwise, a whole family may get up on a certain evening, walk into a restaurant and entrust their lives into the hands of total strangers, the chefs and the stewards in the restaurant and their management.

There are a good number of reasons that will compel an individual to be quite suspicious of a restaurant. First of all, if indeed you must eat there, you may like to see the last medical check-out of the chefs and stewards. The problem created by Typhoid Mary in England is a familiar story for the apostles of preventive as opposed to curative medical practice. [Typhoid Mary a cook by profession, in England, was a carrier of the disease of typhoid fever which led to an epidemic]

An individual walking into a restaurant may therefore wonder: "Does a Typhoid Mary exist in this place?" Rather than sit down to be served, he may first of all walk up to the manager to see the last medical examination report of the staff. Suppose a stool culture for micro organisms was not one of the results in the medical check-out, he may decide that the place is not safe to eat in. He may even go further than that. He may see a stool culture report that read negative, and then wonder about the integrity of the laboratory that examined the sample. So for about half an hour to two hours, he may still be going through the papers of the restaurant. He may find that there is no chest x-ray, and no *Mantoux test (*for *tuberculosis).* God help the manager if any of the staff so much as clears his throat very hard. That may suggest that there may be a carrier of tuberculosis amongst the staff, since chest x-ray results are not available.

Which manager on this earth will tolerate a customer like that? Even the epitomes or fine examples of politeness, great apostles of the business philosophy that preaches that the customer is always right, will find this gentleman and his family a real "*pain in the neck,*" and will be too glad to have the door shut behind them, adding to full measure: "*good riddance to bad rubbish."*

But I have not met a single soul who goes into a restaurant behaving as described above. What is customary is to have whole families sit down, order their meal, eat and go home, no questions asked. The reason is simply that they have faith that the restaurant manager and his staff have taken adequate precautions to ensure that the food is well prepared, and also prepared under standard and acceptable hygienic conditions.

Sometime ago I treated a gentleman who ate fish prepared whole, at a party. It is a favourite dish of party guests in Lagos, Nigeria. He later told me that virtually everybody who ate that fish was hospitalized for acute diarrhoea requiring intravenous infusions of salt solutions popularly known here as *drip*. I have eaten fish prepared in that way several times. That gentleman's experience will not stop me. I doubt that it has stopped him either. He will probably say that that was a *one-off* situation, and there is no way a man can condemn such a delicacy for life.

Natural faith is a part and parcel of daily living. We require it to lead our normal daily lives. We require it to drive a car, eat food, drink water, sit on a chair, fly in an aeroplane, and so on.

Those who do not exercise this natural faith in their daily lives we commonly describe as paranoid personalities. They are afraid of life itself, or many facets of it. We recognize that this may in fact be tell-tale signs of a fundamental mal-adjustment problem or frank psychiatric illness.

It will therefore be quite correct to say that everyone exercises a great measure of natural faith reflexly. In other words they have ceased to stop to ponder in front of a restaurant, when they are about to swallow a capsule, or take some bottled drink. The last time this confidence was shaken was when some tablets were discovered to be laced with cyanide in the USA possibly by a crank. Society went into jitters, and the company knew better than to allow the commodity stay one second longer on the shelves of grocery and pharmacy stores.

If we stop for one moment to analyse the contents of this natural faith, we will discover that what we are describing is faith in human institutions. Society has evolved regulatory bodies to keep control of its activities and ensure that standards are maintained in the various aspects of our social and communal life. So if it is a restaurant, you will rather believe that the licensing authorities have enough integrity to ensure that the restaurant manager or owner has installed the right facilities for storage and preservation of food, cooked and uncooked, and is maintaining minimum standards of hygiene expected in a place like that. So with that at the back of your mind, you simply walk into a place, sit down and eat.

In a society where there is a great deal of awareness and consciousness of basic rights of the individual, a man may walk into a restaurant, and by casual observation sense that the owners are operating below acceptable minimum standards. He may decide to call up the authorities and lodge a formal complaint, hoping that they will get up and do something about it.

There is no way society as we know it today can function otherwise. We are all called to have faith in our institutions, our electricity suppliers, the nuclear accidents notwithstanding, our water supplies and the like. Whenever this faith is shaken, we call on our experts to reassure us that all is still well in spite of all that we are seeing. We are at pains to protect our natural faith in order to preserve ourselves, rather than create a mob of psychological wrecks who have lost faith in society and all her institutions.

It is not often that an individual is called upon to understand the basis of his or her natural faith. We are all often content to trust the words of the experts, once we are satisfied that the expert is associated with a prestigious institution or college that we recognize, or is designated a professor, or world renowned authority.

It is not that we have not been disappointed by experts before. Sometimes we lose faith in their words. But then we never give up on them, not just for their sakes, but for our own sakes as well.

I read the story of the gentleman who advertised for an economist with one hand to work for him. Several amputee-economists showed up, and one of them eventually got hired. Out of curiosity he asked his employer; "Why the emphasis on having one hand?" To which the gentleman quickly replied: "Because I am tired of the advice of those with two hands. They will always say: On the one hand you may do this: but on the other hand you may do that. It always leaves me confused as to what exactly to do." This typifies how much society runs on natural faith, and how much we depend on one another for our daily lives.

So natural faith involves faith in man, in his environment, his institutions which he has established, and the physical order of the universe that he has come to take so much for granted.

When the Bible declares in 2nd Thessalonians chapter 3 and verse 2 that: "...*All men have not faith*," we can see immediately that it cannot be referring to natural faith. We may say without fear of contradiction that all men have natural faith. But the faith that is spiritual, is certainly not available to all men. This was the point the apostle was making in his letter to the Hebrews chapter 4, verse 2, where he said:

> "For indeed the gospel was preached to us as well as unto them; but the word which they heard did not profit them, not being mixed with faith in those who heard them." [NKJ]

The faith that is spiritual is centred on the Almighty God. When an individual harbours and expresses this kind of faith, he tries as much as possible to see the world the way the Almighty God sees it. To put it more succinctly or more precisely, *he sees the world through the eyes of God*. Again without fear of contradiction, I make bold to say that all men certainly do not have this kind of faith. Not all men have this capability or insight to see the world the way God sees it. This was the point the apostle Paul was making in his first letter to the Corinthians chapter 2 and verse 14:

> "But the natural man does not receive the things of the Spirit of God, for they are foolishness to him; nor can he know them, because they are spiritually discerned." [NKJ]

It would appear from this that what the natural man lacks is the capacity to sense the things of the spirit. You may call it spiritual naivety or ignorance. He lacks spiritual insight, and so is incapable of fathoming spiritual truth.

Thus a man that is only natural in his ways is spiritually handicapped. A whole world is totally closed to him. He cannot understand what goes on there, neither can he participate in any way in activities that pertain to the spiritual.

The question is, is it really safe for a man to live this way? Indeed, can an individual afford to live in this way? How dangerous is it to live in this way?

I ask these questions here because sometime ago I had an occasion to discuss with a very brilliant and successful young *entrepreneur* or business woman, who was in the middle of a situation which in my opinion and that of her other friends required a spiritual solution, rather than the physical one we were all offering. After about two hours of discussion, she looked up and said to me: "Look, I know there is God and there is the devil. But I do not have to get involved with any of them. Both of them should just leave me alone to lead my life the way I deem fit," or words to that effect. The question that follows is this; is that sort of indifference to spiritual things really possible?

It might be more fundamental, more basic at least, if not more helpful, to take the question to that level first before returning to look in greater detail at the *Guarantor's Guaranties*. Indeed, a man may prefer to live his life independent of either the Almighty God, or the god of this world, Lucifer. But is that really possible, or is it mere escapism, like the proverbial ostrich that is burying its head in the sand?

Chapter 4

THE SPIRITUAL AND THE NATURAL IN FAITH

It took me quite some time to appreciate that the physical world always obeys the spiritual. The other thing I discovered is that in chronological order, events in the spiritual must antedate events in the physical.

In a lay man's language, this is no other than the law of cause and effect. It may sound extremist to say that nothing actually ever happens by chance, and that what we see as events here are the by-products of the inter-play of spiritual forces, but it is nonetheless true.

Looking at everyday experience to start with, there are many people who would recall sensing things one way or the other, before the events actually took place. One gentleman once dreamt that thieves made away with his car. He woke up agitated and hurriedly went to see if his car parked in front of his house was still there. He was quite relieved to find that it was just a dream. He retired to his bed and slept off again. About four to six weeks later, he actually woke up to find that the car had been removed by unknown persons. It is obvious that the spiritual plot to dispossess him of his property was hatched before the event, and he was sensitive enough to pick-up the signal.

I recall an incident in 1978 while working as a National Youth Service Corp medical officer in the Northern part of Nigeria. I had planned a short weekend trip to the capital city of Lagos in the south by road from my station. Another Christian brother was on the trip with me for company. Just as I was about to get into the car to drive off, the Lord stopped me, and said there was something the matter with the journey, and that I needed to pray. We then went inside, and since we were not quite sure what it was, we decided that the best thing was to pray in tongues and bind all powers of Hell. After about 45 minutes of praying in this way, the Lord spoke again to my heart to the effect that I may now go ahead. I told my companion that all was well again and we left. After about four hours of driving, the first incident occurred. It was to have been a side to side collision with another car and a long trailer. The escape was so miraculous that as we pulled over to top our gas at the gas station, the gentleman in the car behind us pulled over too and was simply shaking his head in utter disbelief. Another three hours of driving, and the second incident occurred. This time it was to have been a head on collision with a lorry that was wrongly overtaking a convoy of vehicles up a grade on a two lane road. Again it was obvious that God had intervened in a very miraculous way to protect me and my companion. The Holy Spirit of God saw the plans of these spiritual plotters, and warned us to deal with them spiritually before we set out on our journey.

It is quite interesting to note that this kind of experience has ample correlation in the word of God, the Bible. This is what has been aptly called, *The Day in Heaven* that must precede *The Day on earth.* Let us pick up the story from the book of Job.

"Now there was a day *(in heaven) when the sons of God came to present themselves before the Lord*, and Satan also came among them.

And the *Lord* said to Satan, From where do you come? So Satan answered the *Lord* and said, From going to and fro on the earth, and from walking back and forth on it.

Then the *Lord* said to Satan, Have you considered my servant Job, that there is none like him on the earth, a blameless and upright man, one who fears God and shuns evil?

So Satan answered the *Lord* and said, Does Job fear God for nothing? Have You not made a hedge around him, around his household, and around all that he has on every side? You have blessed the work of his hands, and his possessions have increased in the land.

But now, stretch out Your hand and touch all that he has, and he will surely curse You to Your face!

So the Lord said to Satan, 'Behold, all that he has is in your power; only do not lay a hand on his person.' Then Satan went out from the presence of God." [Job 1:6-12 NKJ]

What we have here is the day in heaven when a conversation took place between the Lord and Lucifer about Job. The Lord boasted that Job was upright in his ways. The devil said it was not without justification since Job was highly sheltered by the Lord. When the Lord permitted Satan to prove Job's loyalty, the matter of Job's subsequent experiences and fortune was already decided. The day on earth was soon to follow.

"Now there was a day *(on earth)* when his (Job's) sons and daughters were eating and drinking wine in their oldest brother's house; and a messenger came to Job and said, The oxen were ploughing and the donkeys feeding beside them, when the Sabeans raided them and took them away - indeed they have killed the

> servants with the edge of the sword; and I alone have escaped to tell you!
>
> While he was still speaking, another also came and said, The fire of God came from heaven and burned up the sheep and the servants, and consumed them; and I alone have escaped to tell you!
>
> While he was still speaking, another also came and said, The Chaldeans formed three bands, raided the camels and took them away, yes, and killed the servants with the edge of the sword; and I alone have escaped to tell you!
>
> While he was still speaking, another also came and said, Your sons and daughters were eating and drinking wine in their oldest brother's house, and suddenly a great wind came from across the wilderness and struck the four corners of the house, and it fell on the young men, and they are dead; and I alone have escaped to tell you." (Job 1:13-19 NKJ)

Now going by the wishes of this dear friend who appealed to both the Almighty God and Lucifer to leave her alone, it would appear that the issue is just not as simple as that. Take the experience of Daniel in the book of Daniel chapter 10 for instance. He was totally unaware as to what was responsible for the delay in God answering his prayers. QQuite unknown to him, his prayers were answered the moment he prayed. But events in the spiritual realm delayed his receiving the answer for twenty-one days.

> "Then he said to me, "Do not fear, Daniel, for from the first day that you set your heart to understand, and to humble yourself before your God, your words were heard; and I have come because of your words. But the prince of the kingdom of Persia withstood me twenty-one days; and behold, Michael, one of the chief princes, came to help me, for I had been left alone there with the kings of Persia..." [Daniel 10:12-13 NKJ]

To purport to ignore events in the spirit realm, and by that imagine that they would then by-pass you, would amount to nothing more than wishful thinking. Again not to have the capacity to participate in these determinant events in the spirit realm, is a noticeable disadvantage. The experiences of Daniel and Job are quite instructive. Not only were they unaware of these events in the spirit realm, they appeared to be incapable of directly influencing their outcome. The ability of mortal man to get involved in activities in the spirit realm would therefore prove of decided advantage to him.

It would appear that natural faith is of no consequence in this realm, as both Job and Daniel possessed a great deal of it, as successful men in society in their various generations.

In Daniel's experience we learn that persevering prayer proved effective in eliciting arch-angelic intervention, for Michael a chief prince of God abandoned other theatres of activity to intervene here on behalf of Daniel.

As we study the Bible very closely, we will discover that as good as this Daniel's experience is, it is only a second best because he himself could not intervene directly. But if one could intervene directly, using an authority that is well recognised and well respected in the spiritual realm, it certainly would be more preferable. This ability will then confer a right that is hitherto exclusive to spirit beings, to a human being.

The gateway to this authority is the crux of the spiritual type of faith. And we shall proceed to look at this now.

Chapter 5

THE SAVING FAITH

We must address this dimension of faith first, for it is the foundation on which every other faith rests. Faith is the language through which the spirit of man and the Holy Spirit of God communicate with each other. The Bible declares that God is a Spirit in John 4 verse 24. Since no man has seen God at anytime, [John 1:18], then the only way a mortal man can relate with God is by sensing Him through his own spirit, which in turn transmits this signal to the human mind which reaches out with his faith tentacles or faith antenna to pick it up. There is the initial element of uncertainty with respect to the integrity of the communication. But experiences soon dispel the doubts as events in life prove the accuracy of the reception and so the integrity of the communication. We must understand the role that faith plays here. *Spiritual communications because of their inherent intangibility, acquire their greatest import through experience.* We cannot touch or feel the Holy Spirit of God, but we get to sense Him, and with time, we get to know when He is communicating with us. The study of the Bible where God has revealed Himself, as well as the vital principles involved in our relationship with Him, serve as a reference guide or standard with which we judge spiritual communications. It provides the base on which a man can stand by faith to sense these spiritual signals.[*Pathway To Conversational Prayer - Vantage Press N.Y.]

The Bible teaches that, *"The just shall live by faith."* What is implied here is not simply the beginning, but also the continuation. The just shall come alive by faith, and shall continue to stay alive by faith.

When we speak about the saving faith, what is implied is that faith, which enables the individual to make his or her first real contact with the Almighty God *Until a man has received the faith that is unto salvation, he cannot make contact with God. The Bible tells us why.*

> "In reply Jesus declared, I tell you the truth, no one can see the kingdom of God unless he is born again.
>
> "How can a man be born when he is old?" Nicodemus asked. "Surely he cannot enter a second time into his mother's womb to be born!"
>
> Jesus answered, *"I tell you the truth, no one can enter the kingdom of God unless he is born of water and the spirit. Flesh gives birth to flesh, but the Spirit gives birth to Spirit.* You should not be surprised at my saying, You must be born again." [John 3:3-7 NIV]

When an individual receives the faith unto salvation, he becomes a new creation. This is because his or her spirit which hitherto was dead or non-functional, is brought back to life by the activating power of the Spirit of God.

But this process takes place only by faith, as the Bible here tells us.

"For it is by grace you have been saved, through faith - and this not from yourselves, it is the gift of God - not by works, so that no-one can boast." [Ephesians 2:8 and 9]

It is quite important to grasp how this really comes about. The Bible declares in Romans chapter 10, verse 17, that faith comes to an individual when his mind is exposed to the word of God which carries the revelation knowledge of God. Again in Romans chapter 12, verse 3, the Bible declares that God offers this faith to everyone who has believed. In other words, no one can believe in Christ Jesus as the Son of God from Heaven, who came to die for our sins, except he or she receives this *faith quantum* known as *saving faith*. Let us see if we can visualize what happens when an individual is exposed to the preaching of the gospel. The Spirit of the Lord begins to draw him or her to God, using His faith building signals. These faith building signals from the Spirit of God, sensitize their minds, assisting them to recognize truth in what is being preached. Once they do that, and proceed to consent to surrender themselves to the Saviour's cleansing, then the Spirit of God proceeds immediately to quicken their human spirit so that a regular communication channel is established between them. Now the most important thing to grasp here is that not only is this salvation by faith, but also even that faith is a gift which the individual does not deserve.

There are quite a good number of well meaning people who have considerable problems appreciating why salvation should be by faith only. There is undoubtedly the element of human cooperation, evidenced by the individual's consent to surrender to Christ on God's terms, as well as his willingness to accept the necessity of salvation for his soul as absolute truth based on the word of God. But this in no way implies work, since what is being offered cannot be deserved as of merit or as a reward.

But they refer to the writing of James the apostle, and say by implication that works have a great deal to do with salvation too. But the moment we examine the relevant scriptures closely, we are left in no doubt as to the implied meaning of the apostle.

> "What does it profit, my brethren, if someone says he has faith but does not have works? Can faith save him?
>
> If a brother or sister is naked and destitute of daily food, and one of you says to them, Depart in peace, be warmed and filled, but you do not give them the things which are needed for the body, what does it profit? *Thus also faith by itself, if it does not have works is dead.*
>
> But someone will say, You have faith, and I have works. Show me your faith without your works, and I will show you my faith by my works.
>
> You believe that there is one God. You do well. Even the demons believe and tremble.
>
> But do you want to know, O foolish man, that faith without works is dead?
>
> *Was not Abraham our father justified by works, when he offered Isaac his son on the altar? Do you see that faith was working together with his work, and by works, faith was made perfect?*
>
> And the Scripture was fulfilled which says, Abraham believed God, and it was accounted to him for righteousness. And he was called the friend of God.
>
> *You see then that a man is justified by works, and not by faith only.*
>
> Likewise, was not Rahab the harlot also justified by works when she received the messengers and sent them out another way?
>
> *For as the body without the spirit is dead, so faith without works is dead also."* [James 2:14-26]

I have detailed this long passage because it offers so much to us to scrutinize. I have heard people read the passages we have detailed here and say: "This is what I have always said. This Bible is full of contradictions. On the one hand, 'the just shall live by faith only.' Then on the other hand, works are actually more important".

But the moment we begin to examine the passage more closely, we notice that the examples offered by the apostle are most revealing, and go a long way to throw more light on the works themselves.

The works that count unto salvation are the works that faith produces. They are not works that people design themselves, but works that God demands of them through revelation. In this case, the fact that God demanded it of them implies that they had known God, or were spiritually sensitive enough to know in which direction God was moving. So in actual fact, the apostle was referring to works produced by faith in God, through obedience.

I purposely highlighted the case of Abraham above, as a typical example. The fact that Abraham's attempt to sacrifice Isaac was urged specifically by God is not in doubt. The act by itself is abhorred by God. He only used it to determine where Abraham's first loyalty was: to the Almighty God, or to his new found love for his son Isaac. So in actual fact, it is Abraham's faith in God that we are seeing in that work. The work itself would have been awful if God had not urged it. But what made it significant is that it was in response or in obedience to God's command.

For an individual who does not know God, and does not hear God, neither does he listen to God, to pile up works for works sake, will be a very grievous mistake.

The case of Rahab the prostitute is no different. She sensed the way God was moving with these words:

> "I know that the *Lord* has given you the land, that the terror of you has fallen on us, and that all the inhabitants of the land are fainthearted because of you. For we have heard how the *Lord* dried up the water of the Red Sea for you when you came out of Egypt, and what you did to the two kings of the Amorites who were on the other side of the Jordan, Sihon and Og, whom you utterly destroyed. And as soon as we heard these things, our hearts melted; neither did there remain any more courage in anyone because of you, *for the Lord your God, He is God in heaven above and on earth beneath."*
> [Joshua 2:9-11]

The moment Rahab sensed the way the Almighty God was moving, she cast her lot with God and His worshippers. It was a great act of faith. The works that she did subsequently, which in this case was offering protection to the spies from Joshua, an act that is treasonable by itself, only assumes significance because it was a vote on the side of the Almighty God. She was urged in her spirit to seek the favour of the Lord by helping to preserve the true worship of God here on earth which these descendants of Abraham represented, as opposed to the idolatrous and immoral orgies that is the mode of worship of the rest of the people.

So again what we are seeing is not just works for works sake, but works that originated in the spirit, and so must of necessity be by faith, as faith is the only sensor of the spirit.

In the light of all that we have said, we can now re-construct James statements in James 2, 17 and 26 as follows: *Thus also faith,* (by which is meant something that God has urged you in your spirit as a result of the fact that you know God, and you and God hold regular dialogue together; it could also mean something you have read in the Bible which the Lord has urged on you through communication with your human spirit) *if it does not have works,* (by which is meant, if you do not believe what God told you, or where you believe it, you do not go ahead to do what He has urged you in your spirit to do as a result of the personal relationship you share with Him), *is dead* (by which is meant that, the faith is non-existent because you failed to carry out what God has clearly told you. What you have said by implication is that you do not really know God the way a man or woman of faith should know Him, and so your faith relationship with Him does not really exist.)

This is quite different from an individual who sets up his standards of morality, and expects that God will endorse those standards as being sufficient basis for relating with Him.

Indeed, faith without works is dead. It certainly does not exist. For once an individual has a faith relationship with the Almighty God, then it is synonymous with a spirit-centred relationship which implies communion and dialogue. The fundamental tenet or basic principle of that communion is that the Bible is the word of God, and what it says is what God says. [2nd Timothy 3:16,17).

We see therefore how Paul in Ephesians 2 verses 8 and 9, and James in the passage above are saying the same thing.

The apostle Paul went further to put the relationship between faith and works in perspective complementing James. Here it is all over again.

> "For it is by grace you have been saved, through faith- and this not from yourselves, it is the gift of God - not by works, so that no-one can boast. For we are God's workmanship, created in Christ Jesus

to do good works, which God prepared in advance for us to do." [Ephesians 2:8-10 NIV]

What James is saying is that if we fail to do the good works for which we have been created in Christ Jesus, then the implication is that we have not received the saving faith by grace, which means that the faith is dead or does not exist.

The prophet Isaiah says that doing good works as an end in itself, that is, as a basis of acceptance before the Almighty God, is like presenting the Lord with filthy rags. [Isaiah 64:6]

The apostle Paul lamented the tragedy of those who would rather set up their own standards, instead of making do with what the Almighty God has provided in Christ Jesus.

"Brothers, my heart's desire and prayer to God for the Israelites is that they may be saved. For I can testify about them that they are zealous for God, but their zeal is not based on knowledge. Since they did not know the righteousness that comes from God and sought to establish their own, they did not submit to God's righteousness. *Christ is the end of the Law so that there may be righteousness for everyone who believes.*" [Romans 10:1-4 NIV]

Once I had the opportunity to watch a gentleman tangle with the relationship between faith and works in salvation. He contended that justification is by works, and that is why you can never really be sure that you will be saved until you get to heaven. If you get there and you are let in, then what it means is that you had enough good works to let you through. He tried to use the parable of the Tares and the Wheat to justify his position. [Matthew 13:24-30] He contended that since the owner says the tares and the wheat should be separated at the harvest, no one can really say which side he or she will end up.

I have chosen to raise this here because since I first heard it in 1971, I have since heard other people who hold such views. The moment we examine the story, the whole argument collapses. We see immediately that what is waiting till the harvest is not the conversion of tares to wheat, but simply their separation. The tares get to the harvest as tares. The wheat get to the harvest as wheat. If the tares have any spiritual sense, they should know they are tares. The wheat by the same token should know they are wheat. They are growing together in the same field. That we know for sure. I am sure nobody is fooled by the tedium of religion, church membership, alms giving, etc. One does not need to be spiritually alive to do any of these things. However, the moment he or she becomes spiritually alive by faith in the finished work of grace in Christ Jesus, his or her life becomes controlled by the principles and concepts in God's word, and by the Holy Spirit of God, to whom he or she is now tuned, through the quickened human spirit.

Talking about this parable of Tares and Wheat in the gospel of Matthew noted above, it is primarily to ensure that there are no mistakes, that the reaping is reserved for angels who are not liable to make the sort of mistakes that the labourers would have made. The labourers being humans may have been fooled by the seeming similarities between the tares and the wheat, and may have mistakenly called some tares wheat and some wheat tares. But the angels being ministering spirits from the Almighty God, [Hebrews 1:14] have the priviledge of omniscience, and so cannot be thus fooled.

Besides, this parable also leaves the final determination of an individual's status to him or her. Neither the Pastor, the

Evangelist nor the Prophet as labourers in the field, can pronounce you saved or unsaved ultimately. The responsibility is squarely yours to make the decision yourself. If you have made this decision in your lifetime, the reapers, the angels, will surely know when they come for the harvest. If you did not make it, they will equally know.

How to Receive the Saving Grace Through Faith

A man may say, since I was not there when our Lord Jesus Christ walked this earth, how on earth am I supposed to make contact with Him, so I can receive this saving faith through grace?

I suppose this is the sort of question the apostle Paul had in mind when he wrote by the Holy Ghost in Romans chapter 10 from verse 6 to 13.

> "But the righteousness that is by faith says, "Do not say in your heart, Who will ascend into heaven? *(that is, to bring Christ down)* or who will descend into the deep? *(that is to bring Christ up from the dead).* But what does it say? The word is near you; it is in your mouth and in your heart, that is the word of faith we are proclaiming. *That if you confess with your mouth, Jesus is Lord, and believe in your heart that God raised him from the dead, you will be saved. For it is with your heart that you believe and are justified, and it is with your mouth that you confess and are saved.* As the Scripture says, anyone who trusts in him will never be put to shame. For there is no difference between Jew and Gentile - the same Lord is Lord of all and richly blesses all who call on him, *for everyone who calls on the name of the Lord will be saved."* [NIV]

Indeed the word is in the heart and in the mouth of every individual who has heard the message of salvation and redemption through the shed blood of Jesus Christ. Some, after they have heard the word, only stop to argue about it and debate it. Others simply ignore it preferring man made concepts. But for anyone who will humble himself or herself before his or her maker, the eternal law of God and His provisions in grace as stated by the Bible says that:

"The wages of sin is death." [Romans 6:23a] or as Ezekiel chapter 18 and verse 4 put it; *" The soul that sinneth it shall die."*

The grace of God in Christ Jesus provides a substitute sacrifice for the repentant sinner. *"Very rarely will anyone die for a righteous man, though for a good man someone might possibly dare to die. But God demonstrates his own love for us in this: While we were still sinners, Christ died for us."* [Romans 5:7,8 NIV]

Having provided a substitute sacrifice for the sinner, the love and the mercy of God beckons to every man and every woman and says:

"Come now, let us reason together, says the Lord. Though your sins are like scarlet, they shall be as white as snow; though they are red as crimson, they shall be like wool. If you are willing and obedient, you will eat the best from the land; but if you resist and rebel, you will be devoured by the sword." [Isaiah 1:18-20 NIV]

Those who are willing and obedient, and receive the Lord Jesus Christ into their hearts as their Lord and Saviour, or more appropriately as their substitute sacrifice for their many sins for which they deserve to die, are assured that:

"As many as received Him to them he gave the right to become children of God, even to those who believe in His name: who were born, not of blood, nor of the will of the flesh, nor of the will of man, but of God." [John 1:12,13 NKJ]

What is hereby conferred in being a child of God is cardinal to appreciating the dimensions of faith. Implied in the idea of being a child of God, is a quickened spirit, which enables the individual to be able to sense God and communicate with Him.

The Bible declares in Romans 14:23, that *"Whatsoever is not of faith is sin."* The reason for this is that faith is the only language spoken between the quickened spirit of man, and the Spirit of God. So whatsoever is not of faith, was not communicated to man by the Spirit of God, and is consequently outside of the mind of God on the particular situation. It is because the opportunity to have a quickened spirit is open to all men, and whosoever will may come, that the Bible has made such a sweeping generalisation. If you cannot walk by faith, because your spirit is not yet quickened, then you can go ahead and change your spiritual status from death to life, so you can receive the capacity to sense the Spirit of God, and so walk by faith. It is as a result of the fact that faith has a universal application that the apostle Paul declared in 2nd Corinthians chapter 5 and verse 7: *"For we walk by faith, not by sight."* In other words, we have the capacity to sense the Spirit of God all the time and in every situation. We no longer rely on our natural assessment of things and events.

This position is so basic to appreciating and experiencing the various dimensions of faith, and fathoming the rich treasures that walking by faith affords the individual, that we will need to explore it in greater detail.

Chapter 6

THE UNIVERSAL AND THE PARTICULAR IN FAITH

I believe we would benefit quite a bit if we stopped to look briefly at the concept of the universal as opposed to the particular in the faith-walk before God.

Once an individual has been born again, or has accepted Jesus into his heart and life as Lord and Saviour, he enters into a covenant relationship with God. The promises of God in the Bible, become like a personal letter from God to him as a member of the body of Christ, which is His one indivisible church here on earth. This is the point that the apostle Peter was making in his second letter to the Church;

> "Grace and peace be multiplied to you in the knowledge of God and of Jesus our Lord, as His divine power has given to us *all things that pertain to life and godliness,* through the knowledge of Him who called us by glory and virtue, by which have been given to us *exceedingly great and precious promises, that through these you may be partakers of the divine nature*, having escaped the corruption that is in the world through lust." [2nd Peter 1:2-4 NKJ]

This passage underscores the universality of the promises of God. They without exception have been bequeathed to us, and they concern all things that pertain to life, which includes ordinary everyday living, and all things that pertain to godliness which includes our daily spiritual walk. They contain exceedingly great and precious promises. If we progressively appropriate these promises, we shall be more and more like God our Father everyday by becoming more and more like His Son Jesus Christ our Lord and Saviour.

This is a daunting challenge and a daunting ambition. Knowing how Jesus walked this earth, expressing the complete life of God by the Holy Spirit totally, without limitation or hindrance of any kind, whether internal or external, we recognize that we do have a challenge before us. But only a challenge, because Jesus had already told us as members of His body:

> "Verily, verily, I say unto you, He that believeth on me, the works that I do shall he do also; and greater works than these shall he do; because I go unto my Father." [John 14:12 KJV]

John the Baptist expressed our Lord Jesus Christ's abiding unity with the Godhead in these words:

"For he whom God hath sent speaketh the words of God: for God giveth not the Spirit by measure unto him." [John 3:34 KJV]

And Jesus went further to tell us, that we share in this unity with the Father once we believe in Him as saviour and Lord.

"At that day you shall know that I am in my Father, and ye in me, and I in you." [John 14:20 KJV]

In spite of all these we are confronted by apostles James abiding observation:

> "Where do wars and fights come from among you? Do they not come from your desires for pleasure that war in your members? You lust and do not have. You murder and covet and cannot obtain. You fight and war. Yet you do not have because you do not ask. You ask and do not receive, because you ask amiss, that you may spend it on your pleasures." [James 4:1-3 NKJ]

What all these tell us is that although all the promises are there for all of us, all the time, in a universal sense, the individual in appropriating each specific promise, must be guided in the particular, with respect to *attitudes, timing, motive, capacity for utilisation, etcetera*, all factors which come under what we will describe as *the will of God in the material time under consideration.*

Let us take a universal promise like the one found in Philippians 4:19, as an example.

"And my God shall supply all your need according to His riches in glory by Christ Jesus." [NKJ]

Indeed, my God, writes the apostle Paul by the Holy Ghost, shall supply all your needs from His rich store house. But contextually, that promise was directed in the particular to those who were giving their material substance for the support of the work of the gospel of our Lord Jesus Christ: those who were giving sacrificially even beyond what was expected of them, (2nd Corinthians 8:1-5) for the support of the great work of evangelisation of the unreached: those who were burdened by the demands of the great commission of our Lord Jesus Christ to go into all the world, and make disciples of all nations.

An individual may give nothing for the spread of the Gospel, care nothing about the Great Commission, sow no seed unto eternity, and yet desire to hold God to the promise of this passage. If he or she receives anything at all, it will be in response to the grace of God in their lives specifically, which takes into consideration their level of growth and maturity in the Lord, and their potential and progress in the Holy Spirit's school of discipleship. Such an experience should not be extrapolated by another individual or it may lead to frustration. In other words you cannot use such a peculiar experience as a basis to determine how the Lord will respond to you.

This is because such an experience lacks predictability since it is obviously personal to the individual. But what will be universal, will be for an individual to live like those who received that promise lived, with a great burden in their heart for the spread of the gospel, giving of their time, money, intellect, skills, etc. for the extension of the kingdom of God in the hearts of men and women. Then they may present their needs to the Lord expecting Him to meet all their needs from His great storehouse.

Still, the appropriateness of each need presented, in the context of the life of the individual in the material time under consideration, is a vital factor. In other words, *"My God shall supply all your need:"* but is He willing to supply this particular need at this particular time?

This was the question James addressed in the passage quoted earlier. If the need is a lust after pleasure, then it may not be met in the life of the individual at that particular time. It is important to emphasize the period, because these factors change.

I recall with a chuckle, one of the stories my father used to tell us.

There was this cobbler who worked on the ground floor studio of a house owned by a wealthy business man who happened to live on the first floor with his family. The rich man had noted with longing, the cobbler's merry and cheerful ways. Each time a passer-by hailed him: "Shoemaker, how are you?" He will respond loudly, "Fine thank you," and will often sing through the whole working day. He envied the cobbler his merry ways, and decided to reward him for adding some mirth and sunshine to the environment.

He invited him to his living room, and gave him a gift of four hundred pounds, which will be something like Ten thousand naira today. Then a strange thing happened afterwards. He noticed after a few days, that he was no longer hearing the cobbler's songs. The gusty replies were no longer heard. After about two weeks, the cobbler was hardly at work any more, and all the singing had gone. But four weeks later, the cobbler was back in his living room with an envelope. He was relieved, and wanted to find out what the problem was. The cobbler said, "Sir, ever since you gave me this money, I have not rested. Anywhere I go, I feel somebody may be raiding my house to steal it. I never can get my mind away from the money no matter how I try. So I have decided to return the money to you rather than let it kill me."

We have a local proverb here that says, that a young man who fails to attain the appropriate age or stature before going for a particular title, here described as tying a loin cloth in-between the legs, the wind will carry him and the cloth away.

The Holy Spirit understands all these factors in the life of an individual very well, and structures their development in His school of discipleship in a comprehensive way. The implication of course is that a need met today may prove detrimental to the spiritual progress of an individual, but the same may not be true tomorrow, after he or she has spent more time or learnt more lessons in this one school of discipleship which every believer is in, whether they recognize it or not.

An individual cannot determine by himself the absolute appropriateness of meeting a particular need in his or her life at a particular time. In other words, you cannot simply say: "Oh the only reason why this need is not met, is because it is not yet God's time for it to be met." If that were to be so, then the question would be, when did you make that discovery? Was it before, or after the request was not met? If it was before, then why did you make it? If it was after, then you would need to be sure that this is not mere unbelief or lack of faith. In other words, if a need is delayed in time, the only person qualified to say the reason why, is the Holy Spirit. The individual can get to know this, through conversational prayer. (See Pathway To Conversational Prayer - Vantage Press NY.)

It will be important to add that failure to recognize the vital place of the concept of the universal and the particular in a man's faith-walk with the Lord, may lead to a lot of heartache and frustration as the individual struggles to fathom or understand why some prayer needs are yet to be answered, or why some answers are 'yes' rather than the 'no' that we are expecting, or *vice versa.*

You would have recognized I am sure that at the centre of all this discourse is the dominant place of *the will of GOD in the life of an individual in time and place.* This is what determines God's response to a prayer request ultimately. We will allude to this frequently as we discuss the various dimensions of faith.

Chapter 7

THE THREE STAGES OF A CHRISTIAN'S WALK OF FAITH

There are three recognisable stages of development in the life of a child of God. The first is soon after he moves from the kingdom of darkness into the kingdom of God. The apostle Peter referred to this as the stage of *Spiritual Babyhood,* where he said: *"As Newborn Babes, desire the pure milk of the word, that you may grow thereby." [1st Peter 2:2 NKJ]*

Then follows this stage of growth, where the individual undergoes progressive transformation through a careful study of the word of God, and a consistent application of the principles of godliness contained therein. We may call this the *Maturation Stage.* Writing to the Romans, the apostle Paul urged them to go on to this maturation through transformation, which will assist them to determine what is that good, acceptable and perfect will of God.

> "And do not be conformed to this world, but be transformed by the renewing of your mind, that you may prove what is that good and acceptable and perfect will of God." [Romans 12:2 NKJ]

In the book of Hebrews chapter 5, the Bible decries the attitude of those who have failed to make any spiritual progress, which is referred to as those who are in a position to eat strong meat, meaning those who by reason of use or practice, have their senses exercised to distinguish good from evil.

> "In fact, though by this time you ought to be teachers, you need someone to teach you the elementary truths of God's word all over again. You need milk, not solid food! Anyone who lives on milk, being still an infant, is not acquainted with the teaching about righteousness. But solid food is for the *Mature*, who by constant use have trained themselves to distinguish good from evil." [Hebrews 6:12-14 NIV]

The third stage is the *Mature Stage* when one has learnt a considerable number of principles that guide a man's walk with his God. This is the stage when a great deal of shadows have disappeared leaving the realities behind, and instilling thereby some hard core lessons that prove quite useful in time. The apostle Paul in his writings to the Philippian church alluded to his expectations of these mature Christians in different situations particularly when there is a divergence of views on issues. He expects them for instance to sift the essentials from the non-essentials, and emphasize the unifying power of accepted common grounds. This is the way he put it while referring to his uncompromising pursuit of the excellency of the high calling of God in Christ Jesus.

"All of us who are Mature should take such a view of things. And if on some point you think differently, that too God will make clear to you. Only let us live up to what we have already attained." [Philippians 3:15-16 NIV]

We may find a striking similarity between these three stages of the Christian life and the experience of the children of Israel on their way from Egypt to Canaan.

The *first stage* will then represent the *exodus from Egypt*, the land of slavery, where man was in bondage to sin and the devil. The crossing of the Red Sea, will then represent the new birth experience that marks a break with or freedom from the bondage to sin and the religious systems of the world around. Embodied within this is the concept of separation: *"Wherefore come out from among them, and be ye separate, saith the Lord, and touch not the unclean thing; and I will receive you." [2nd Corinthians 6:17 KJV]*

Then follows the *second stage*, which is the wilderness experience where growth and maturation is supposed to take place. It is in the wilderness that we learn to walk with God and follow Him, through all the obstacles that may confront us. It is there that we are prepared for Canaan the land of promise, where those who have learnt to walk by faith in its various dimensions, can enter into a continuing rest. In Canaan we will expect to meet with giants and mountains, as well as hostile neighbours; but the mature men and women of faith, know both in theory and by experience, that *with God all things are possible.*

The *third stage* will therefore represent Canaan the land of rest, where these mature men and women grapple with obstacles all around by faith, while they themselves remain at rest. This is analogous to the experience of Jesus who was asleep in the middle of a raging storm. (Mark 4:37-38)

It is because of these various stages of spiritual development in the life of a Christian, that we dare to speak of these dimensions of faith. These dimensions represent wilderness lessons, which come on very handy when we face the giants and the mountains of Canaan.

We may proceed now to look at the Honeymoon faith, which as the name implies, is the experience we have soon after we are born again.

Chapter 8

THE HONEYMOON FAITH

A young man went to the late Pastor S.G. Elton during my undergraduate days, and told him how the Lord always answered his prayers. The old man re-told the story during one of our seminar sessions.

"Let me tell you why the Lord hurries to answer you." We were all very eager to find out. "It is because you are a baby." We were all disappointed. "The Lord always says, hurry and answer them before they fall. But let me tell you," his voice crackled, "it won't always be like that. One day you would have to grow up."

There are many Christians who will remember what I have chosen here to call, the honeymoon faith-walk with the Lord. I recall a young man in those days getting up to testify that he had absolutely no problems. God always answered all his prayers so quickly, and he had absolutely no worries. He wondered for good measure why many people always talked about their problems. Each time I remember this testimony, I remember Pastor Elton's timely warning. *"One day you will have to grow up."*

Indeed, a close look at the experience of the children of Israel, will be quite instructive. When you look at Exodus chapter 15, you can sense in the song of jubilation the great ecstasy they experienced at their miraculous deliverance from the oppression of Pharaoh. They had entered the honeymoon of faith.

> "Then sang Moses and the children of Israel this song unto the Lord, and spake, saying, *I will sing unto the Lord for He has triumphed gloriously: the horse and his rider hath He thrown into the sea.* The Lord is my strength and song, and he is become my salvation: he is my God, and I will prepare him an habitation; my father's God, and I will exalt him. The Lord is a man of war: The Lord is his name." [Exodus 15:1-3 KJV]

The miracle of deliverance from slavery in Egypt, created the euphoria, beneath which was practically nothing of substance. It is no wonder then, that barely two weeks after leaving Egypt, they were ready to return. Hear their murmuring.

> "And the whole congregation of the children of Israel murmured against Moses and Aaron in the wilderness.
>
> And the children of Israel said unto them, Would to God we had died by the hand of the Lord in the land of Egypt, when we sat by the flesh pots, and when we did eat bread to the full; for ye have brought us forth into this wilderness, to kill this whole congregation with hunger." [Exodus 16:2-3 KJV]

During the honeymoon phase of our Christian experience, faith is very thin or shall we say very shallow. The slightest pressure, and the slightest inconvenience forces us to rethink our new found way of life. But in spite of this lack of faith, the answers come anyway, as in this case.

> "Then said the Lord unto Moses, Behold, I will rain bread from heaven for you; and the people shall go out and gather a certain rate everyday, that I may prove them, whether they will walk in my law, or no." [Exodus 16:4 KJV]

But then we may wonder, why do the answers come anyway? The reason is quite obvious. The people do not know God, so not much is expected of them. God is at His in-put stage, to provide the experience that He will use to build-up their faith in Him.

But it is for the same reason that some of us, not realizing that this is a phase only, come under tremendous psychological pressure, trying to find out what has happened to us and our relationship with God. As we meet more and more obstacles in the wilderness, and the answers come a little more slowly than previously, we begin to murmur and grumble and complain. Initially God tolerates our ignorance and lack of faith, as in the case of the children of Israel, but soon those who refuse to grow up and learn to trust the Lord, discover that the Lord is somewhat displeased.

Failure to recognize the honeymoon faith for what it is does create problems. Some honeymoons last for a very long time, and there are certain factors that go to ensure this. One of these is *a child-like simplicity in our faith-walk before the Lord.* This was the point that Jesus was making in Mark chapter 10 and verse 15, about our receiving the kingdom of God like a little child. Those who maintain that child-like simplicity of faith after they have entered the kingdom, do have a long honeymoon.

I would never forget this testimony given by a 10 year old girl in a school I visited in 1973. It was customary for Christian undergraduates to visit students in secondary schools or high schools. I had gone there to share a message on the second coming of Christ.

This little girl asked us to praise the Lord with her for a miracle that took place the previous day. She had a piece of paper stuck in one of her ears, as she played with a friend.

She got alarmed, and asked her friend to help pull it out, but the more she tried the deeper the paper went. After several attempts, she asked her to stop, that Jesus will get it out for her.

After supper, she retired to her bed, and said a simple prayer. "Dear Lord Jesus, I have a piece of paper in my ear. Please help me bring it out. Thank you." She slept off, and woke up in the morning to find the piece of paper on her pillow. It has stayed with me ever since.

The other vital factor that makes honeymoons last a long time is *honesty*. Once we do not pretend to be what we are not, but rather strive to be what we ought to be, then the honeymoon will last a long time. The necessary fallout from this is that we will seek to know the things we are not sure of, and go to any and every length to bridge the gap created by our ignorance of the word of God, and His ways.

The third vital factor is an *insatiable hunger for the truth in God's word*. This is what will prepare us for life in Canaan, where we are supposed to rest in the midst of giants and mountains. This is the rest of faith as Hebrews chapter 4 verses 3, and 11, tell us:

"For we which have believed do enter into rest...

Let us labour therefore to enter into that rest, lest any man fall after the same example of unbelief." [KJV]

Consciousness of these three factors not only make for a long honeymoon, they also ensure a short wilderness trip. However, it is in the wilderness experience itself, which we may call *the school of faith*, that we really learn to enter into rest.

Chapter 9

THE SCHOOL OF FAITH

The experience of the children of Israel in the wilderness offers us a great opportunity to study the nature of events and lessons in the school of faith. It offers us insight into the ways of God, which the prophet Isaiah declares in Isaiah chapter 55 and verse 8, are not the same as our ways. *"For my thoughts are not your thoughts, neither are your ways my ways, saith the Lord."* *[KJV]*

The more we study these experiences in detail, the more light is shed on our experiences as Christians, and the more we are able to appreciate the walk of an individual before God.

One striking lesson that emerges, is that the curriculum for an individual's training in the school of faith is unique to the individual. In other words the content of Mr. A's training programme, may not be the same as that of Mr. B. This is because the content of the programme itself is designed to reflect the lessons the individual will need to learn and assimilate in order to progressively conform to the image of Christ, the perfect man. This is what is responsible for the great differences in individual experiences as Christians, and also the differences in the events we witness as observers or as active participants in our circumstances.

We have already noted that the children of Israel murmured when they were confronted with their first obstacle in Exodus chapter 15. The Lord replied with Manna and quails.

Soon after they finished with the problem of food, came the problem of water in Exodus chapter 17. Their response was no different from the previous.

> "And the people thirsted there for water; and the people murmured there against Moses, and said, Wherefore is this that thou hast brought us up out of Egypt, to kill us and our children and our cattle with thirst? And Moses cried unto the Lord, saying, What shall I do unto this people? they be almost ready to stone me." [Exodus 17:3-4 KJV]

Knowing that they were only babies in their experience of the Almighty God, He answered them again even in their unbelief.

> "And the Lord said unto Moses, Go on before the people, and take with thee of the elders of Israel; and thy rod wherewith thou smotest the river, take in thy hand, and go. Behold, I will stand before thee there upon the rock in Horeb; and thou shalt smite the rock, and there shall come water out of it, that the people may drink. And Moses did so in the sight of the elders of Israel." [Exodus 17:6-7 KJV]

One vital lesson about the school of faith which one can immediately see, is that *students do not device solutions to problems; they simply state the problem as it is, and await instructions from the Lord.* As we shall see subsequently, the ability to internalize this lesson and make it like our second nature, will determine the fruitfulness of each student not only in the school, or in the wilderness but also in Canaan, the land of rest, where mountains and giants as well as hostile neighbours wait to see what we had learnt in the school.

Another vital lesson we see, is that *students also discover solutions by learning from experience,* like Moses and the people did in the war against Amalek, recorded in Exodus chapter 17, verses 8 to 13.

> "And it came to pass, when Moses held up his hand, that Israel prevailed: and when he let down his hand, Amalek prevailed. But Moses' hands were heavy; and they took a stone, and put it under him, and he sat thereon; and Aaron and Hur stayed up his hands, the one on the one side, and the other on the other side; and his hands were steady until the going down of the sun. And Joshua discomfited Amalek and his people with the edge of the sword." [Exodus 17:11-14 KJV]

What they learnt here from experience is that when hands are lifted up continuously in intercession to the Lord, as typified by Moses' uplifted arms, the power of the Lord comes down to intervene to ensure victory for His people. Where intercession is discontinued, then the victory is in jeopardy. Recognizing the vital place of intercession in ensuring victory, Moses solicits the assistance of Aaron and Hur in order to keep the intercessory arms permanently uplifted until victory was won.

Another vital lesson we learn in the school of faith, is *the place of counsel by other students,* albeit those who by reason of age and experience, reflect greater wisdom than us. One fact that emerges clearly is how these counsellors should phrase their counsel, recognizing that they do not have the final say on the matter. This is clearly illustrated in the counsel that Moses' father-in-law gave him with respect to how to administer the nation of Israel in the wilderness. Moses being a typical "DIY-person," (*do it yourself*) was leader, judge, and administrator all in one, for all the people. Jethro thought his method of administration was outrageous, and that he needed to learn the vital lesson of delegation, which decentralizes power alright, but makes for greater efficiency. Delegation will force us to recognize others who are also worthy of trust, and so could be charged with some of our responsibilities, freeing us therefore to concentrate on other areas with greater and better results.

> "Now listen, and let me give you a word of advice, and God will bless you: Be these people's lawyer - their representative before God -bringing him their questions to decide; you will tell them his decisions, teaching them God's laws, and showing them the principles of godly living. Find some capable, godly, honest men who hate bribes, and appoint them as judges, one judge for each 1,000 people; he in turn will have ten judges under him, each in charge of a hundred; and under each of them will be two judges, each responsible for the affairs of fifty people; and each of these will have five judges beneath him, each counselling ten persons. Let these men be responsible to serve the people with justice at all times. Anything that is too important or complicated can be brought to you. But the smaller matters they can take care of themselves. That way it will be easier for you because *YOU WILL SHARE THE BURDEN WITH THEM*. If you follow this advice, and *IF THE LORD AGREES*, you will be able to endure the pressures, and there will be peace and harmony in the camp.
>
> *Moses listened to his father-in-law's advice, and followed this suggestion."* [Exodus 18:19-24 LB]

As a student in this school of faith, Moses learnt the vital lesson of *sharing the burden.* Jethro was careful to remind him though, that he has the responsibility to ascertain that God Almighty who has the final say in every decision, and every innovation, also agrees.

As we study the experiences of the people of Israel, one thing that is striking is that students are often not aware when they are in for a crucial examination or review, which we may refer to as *the day of reckoning*. These reviews are usually not announced ahead of time, and they often begin rather very ordinarily. One case in point is Moses' forty day sojourn in the mountain of God, Mount Sinai, to collect the written decalogue or the ten commandments which had earlier been spoken to the people at the foot of the mountain by God. This sojourn was preceded by a demonstration of the awesome power of God before the people.

The test is revealed in the fact that the exercise took so long to accomplish, *giving sufficient time for the people to be left on their own to prove them*. What was in question was whether their various experiences of the reality of God so far, was sufficient to keep them away from reverting to idol or fetish worship.

The score was a woeful zero.

"And the Lord said unto Moses, Come up to me into the mount, and be there: and I will give thee tables of stone, and a law, and commandments which I have written; that thou mayest teach them. And Moses rose up, and his minister Joshua: and Moses went up into the mount of God.

And he said unto the elders, Tarry ye here for us, until we come again unto you: and, behold, Aaron and Hur are with you: if any man have any matters to do, let him come unto them. And Moses went up into the mount, and a cloud covered the mount.

And Moses went into the midst of the cloud, and gat him up into the mount: and Moses was in the mount forty days and forty nights." [Exodus 24:12-15 & 18 KJV]

This is the setting of their test or review, and here is their performance.

"And when the people saw that Moses delayed coming down from the mountain, the people gathered together to Aaron, and said to him, Come, make us gods that shall go before us; for as for this

Moses, the man who brought us up out of the land of Egypt, we do not know what has become of him. And Aaron said to them, Break off the golden earrings which are in the ears of your wives, your sons and your daughters, and bring them to me. So all the people broke off the golden earrings which were in their ears, and brought them to Aaron. And he received the gold from their hand, and he fashioned it with an engraving tool, and made a moulded calf. Then they said, This is your god, O Israel, that brought you out of the land of Egypt!" [Exodus 32:1-4 NKJ]

As far as the people were concerned, Moses was the symbol of this God that speaks with and through thunder and lightening and clouds of smoke. When Moses disappeared for what looked like an unending or interminable period, the people felt they needed an object of worship, which their natural senses could appreciate.

As we study this review we begin to appreciate patterns that are easily discernible in our everyday experience.

Why, for instance, did Moses stay so long? Was he not aware that the people did not know God that well to last that long without him? He should have known better. Anybody could have predicted the outcome, especially as the people were inclined to return to Egypt each time they faced an obstacle.

But the crux of the matter is that the Teacher in this one school of faith, decided that the people were sufficiently exposed to take what was coming to them, particularly with their exposure to the awesome powers of the Almighty God, just before Moses ascended the mountain. That impression was designed to last a life time. That it did not last forty days is not the fault of the Teacher. Anyone who is a teacher or has been a teacher will agree. Weekly lessons are usually followed in this part of the world by weekly assignments, and the system of continuous assessment ensures that every weekly assignment counts in the final evaluation.

The anger of God at this abysmal performance can only best be imagined.

> "And the Lord said to Moses, I have seen this people, and indeed it is a stiff-necked people! Now therefore, let Me alone, that My wrath may burn hot against them and I may consume them. And I will make of you a great nation." [Exodus 32:10 NKJ]

This kind of review that the people experienced here is quite common in the experience of Christians. The issue can be resolved into this one question: "Given the opportunity to return into the world and renounce your faith in our Lord Jesus Christ as Lord and Saviour, what will you do?" Sometimes the situation that brings this question about is a combination of factors that subject the individual to intense pressures.

The school of faith is designed to instil the lesson of ultimate victory or triumph of God. It is designed to teach us that darkness can only be for a time, and that faith in the goodness of the Almighty God, faith in His awesome power and might which He is ready and willing to release on our behalf in due time, will always cause us to triumph in *ALL* situations, over any and every adversary. *It is only a matter of time, and the Lord will arise and all His enemies in our lives and circumstances will scatter.*

This is the overall vital lesson we are supposed to learn in the school of faith in the wilderness.

- We are made to experience the deliverance of the Almighty God in various circumstances.

- We are taught how it works, and how to bring it about.

- We are taught the things that we do or say that hinder it, and attitudes that we may harbour which send the wrong signals about our spiritual progress to heaven.

- We are made to see that *we are born to win*. The wilderness is only there to teach us how to live victoriously everyday.

- We are taught through practical lessons that the devil through men and circumstances will throw several obstacles on our path of spiritual, and material as well as physical progress. But that it is our responsibility to learn how to stop him in every way.

- Initially we receive a great deal of assistance as babies that are carried. But then we are taught to stand on our two feet, and *fight the good fight of faith*.

There are more lessons that emerge in the school of faith. They include the following:

- That the battleground for the fight of faith is the heart of man, where the conflict is principally whether to believe God and have absolute and unshakable confidence in our triumph over our enemies through *His awesome powers in us* [Ephesians 3:20] or to fix our minds on our circumstances and so become despondent and blame God for our misfortunes.

- We are taught that the obstacles we encounter in our lives is our call to battle, not with the circumstances themselves, but with the unseen powers that produce them.

- We are taught in the school of faith that so long as we know that victory is always ours, then we should *always have this victory in us whenever we come face to face with any obstacle or challenge.*

Other very vital lessons emerge in the school of faith, and these include the following:

* Those who do not have this victory inside them, cannot have it outside them in their circumstances.

* Anyone who has lost the battle of faith in his heart, has already lost that battle in his life and circumstances. We fight and win inside before we can win outside.

* The release of power from the throne room of the Almighty God, to back up the authority exercised by His children, is dictated by the signal that is coming from inside them.

* Those whose hearts are thrilled by the smell of victory at the beginning of any battle, draw tremendous power from the throne room of God to back-up the authority they exercise on earth in their lives and circumstances.

The children of Israel were to learn these lessons painfully in the wilderness, at the borders of Canaan.

Indeed there is tremendous power in God for all His children. The school of faith is designed to teach us how to draw from it, as we exercise authority on God's behalf here on earth.

It is there that we are taught the things that help, and the things that hinder the exercise of that power.

* We may note however, that it is only those who perform well in the school of faith, that qualify for

Canaan. The rest are left to languish in the wilderness, never to experience the rest that faith brings across the Jordan river of life.

As they approached the borders of Canaan, the children of Israel were unaware that they were in for their qualifying examination. They were unaware that the Lord was about to make a separation between those who will languish in the wilderness of life, and those who have learnt enough faith to go on to their rest in Canaan. This was an appraisal that was based on their performance so far, and their performance at this crucial review.

Here is how this examination was conducted.

> "And the Lord spoke to Moses, saying, Send out men to spy the land of Canaan, which I am giving to the children of Israel; from each tribe of their fathers you shall send a man, every one a leader among them. So Moses sent them from the Wilderness of Paran according to the command of the Lord all of them who were heads of the children of Israel." [Numbers 13:1-3 NKJ]

As these men were about to leave, Moses gave them this charge:

> "...Go up this way into the South, and go up to the mountains, and see what the land is like: whether the people who dwell in it are strong or weak, few or many; whether the land they dwell in *is good or bad*; whether the cities they inhabit are like camps or strongholds; whether the land is rich or poor; and whether there are forests there or not. Be of good courage. And bring some of the fruit of the land..." [Numbers 13:17-20]

In the charge that Moses gave to the people, a number of vital lessons emerge.

The spies were to go and assess the obstacles that will confront the people in Canaan.

The obvious implication of this vital lesson in the school of faith, is that students are not called to ignore their realities. If anything, they are called to appraise their realities, and assess them comprehensively, their positive and negative attributes as they relate to their objective. "Assess the Land," Moses charged them, "and when you come back, let us know what your findings are, the pros and the cons."

It is quite instructive to study the report brought back by the spies. What we see immediately is that the report can be divided into two: *the facts as they are,* and then *the interpretation given to those facts.* Let us look at the facts;

> "So they departed and came back to Moses and Aaron and all the congregation of the children of Israel in the Wilderness of Paran, at Kadesh; they brought back word to them and to all the congregation, and showed them the fruit of the land.
>
> Then they told him and said: We went to the land where you sent us. It truly flows with milk and honey, and this is its fruit.
>
> Nevertheless, the people who dwell in the land are strong; the cities are fortified and very large; moreover we saw the descendants of Anak there. The Amalekites dwell in the land of the South; the Hittites, the Jebusites, and the Amorites dwell in the mountains; and the Canaanites dwell by the sea and along the banks of the Jordan." [Numbers 13:26-29 NKJ]

As far as the report of the facts was concerned, all the spies were in agreement. Facts are facts, and students in the school of faith are taught to recognize the facts for what they are, reality. But they are also taught that facts today, do not often determine ultimate reality. It is in the versions of the interpretation of these facts and what they mean to the objective of the people, (ie. rest in Canaan) that the lessons of the school of faith shine forth.

> "Then Caleb quieted the people before Moses, and said, Let us go up at once and take possession, *for we are well able to overcome it.*" [Numbers 13:30 NKJ]

Caleb's interpretation of the facts was that they did not constitute any obstacle to the achievement of their objective. But others, with the exception of Joshua, thought differently.

> "But the men who had gone up with him said, We are not able to go up against the people, for they are stronger than we. And they gave the children of Israel a bad report of the land which they had spied out, saying; The land through which we have gone as spies is a land that devours its inhabitants, and all the people whom we saw in it are men of great stature. There we saw the giants (the descendants of Anak came from the giants); and *we were like grasshoppers in our own sight*, and so we were in their sight." [Numbers 13:31-33 NKJ]

As we look at the second interpretation, we are confronted with a rather different perception of the facts. Caleb said, "let us go immediately and take possession. We can do it." The others said, "Oh no we can't." The question is, "What is the basis of Caleb's confidence?" And one may rightly wonder also, how on earth those people came by their own conclusion. It is bad enough that they were like grasshoppers in their own eyes, but how did they find out that the people also regarded them as grasshoppers.

An individual is allowed to have any perception of himself based on his or her assessment of a situation. But unless he confronts another person directly, he or she cannot be categorical about the other person's perception of him or her. Indeed, the spies may call themselves grasshoppers. But who told them that the giants were also calling them grasshoppers? Spies are sent to observe rather stealthily, not to conduct an opinion poll.

But which of these two reports should a congregation accept, since the spies were only representing the larger body? The more sensible thing to do, would be to ask each party to discuss the basis of their confidence or lack of it. But on this occasion, the people chose to decide on the side of the bad report.

> "Then all the congregation lifted up their voices and cried, and the people wept that night. And all the children of Israel murmured against Moses and Aaron, and the whole congregation said to them, If only we had died in the land of Egypt! Or if only we had died in this wilderness! Why has the Lord brought us to this land to fall by the sword, that our wives and children should become victims? Would it not be better for us to return to Egypt? So they said to one another, Let us select a leader and return to Egypt." [Numbers 14:1-4 NKJ]

When the people made this decision, Joshua and Caleb decided it was time to justify their confidence before the people. They got up and said to the people:

> "The land we passed through to spy out is an exceedingly good land. *If the Lord delights in us, then He will bring us into this land and give it to us,* a land which flows with milk and honey. Only *do not rebel against the Lord, nor fear the people of the land,* for they are our bread; their protection has departed from them, AND THE LORD IS WITH US. Do not fear them." [Numbers 14:7-9 NKJ]

Joshua and Caleb, stated the basis of their confidence: *The Lord is with us*. This is faith, learnt from the wilderness' school of faith.

They also stated the basis of the other groups lack of confidence: *fear and rebellion,* implying thereby, that although they all were in the same school, these men had failed to learn vital lessons of a man's walk before the Almighty God.

But what was the peoples' response to all these:

"And all the congregation said to stone them with stones"

When we look at the Lord's response to this development, we notice immediately that the days of pampering were over. It is as if He was saying to these people: "Look! you have been here in this school long enough to show better performance. Since you have failed woefully, you will now bear the consequences of your failure to reflect the lessons taught you in the school of faith."

> "And the Lord said to Moses: How long will this people reject me? And how long will they not believe Me, with all the signs which I have performed among them? I will strike them with a pestilence and disinherit them, and I will make of you a nation greater and mightier than they." [Numbers 14:11-12 NKJ]

Moses started immediately to intercede for the people. All his efforts served only to postpone the immediate execution of the death penalty imposed on them, and convert it to what looks like a life sentence.

> "Then the Lord said: I have pardoned according to your word; but truly, as I live, all the earth shall be filled with the glory of the Lord - because all these men who have seen My glory and the signs which I did in Egypt and in the wilderness, and have put me to the test now these ten times, and have not heeded My voice, they certainly shall not see the land of which I swore to their fathers, nor shall any of those who rejected Me see it.
>
> But My servant Caleb, because he has a different spirit in him and has followed Me fully, I will bring into the land where he went, and his descendants shall inherit it." [Numbers 14:20-24 NKJ]

Rather than proceed to their land of rest, the Lord ordered that the people should wander in the wilderness for their infidelity. He however singled out Joshua and Caleb because they reflected a grasp of the basic lessons of the school of faith.

> *"Now the Amalekites and the Canaanites dwell in the valley; tomorrow turn and move out into the wilderness by the Way of the Red Sea"*
>
> Say to them, As I live says the Lord, just as you have spoken in My hearing, so I will do to you: *The carcasses of you who have murmured against Me shall fall in this wilderness, all of you who were numbered, according to your entire number, from twenty years old and above. Except for Caleb the son of Jephunneh and Joshua the son of Nun,* you shall by no means enter the land which I swore I would make you dwell in. *But your little ones whom you said would be victims, I would bring in, and they shall know the land which you have despised.* But as for you, your carcasses shall fall in this wilderness. And your sons shall be shepherds in the wilderness forty years, and bear the brunt of your infidelity, until your carcasses are consumed in the wilderness. *According to the number of the days in which you spied out the land, forty days, for each day you shall bear your guilt one year, namely forty years, and you shall know My rejection."* [Numbers 14:25,28-34 NKJ]

As we study this experience in the school of faith, we are made to shudder at the grave consequences pronounced here by the Almighty God. His tolerance of their unbelief appears to have run out completely. They had failed to respond correctly on ten occasions. In other words, *they had ten examinations, and flunked every single one of them.* They had hoped that this exam or test was just like the previous, and if they showed signs of repentance, the Lord would forgive them, and things would be back to normal again. But this was their last chance. Moses had occasion to point out to them the great difference there is between *faith* and *presumption.*

> *"Then Moses told these words to all the children of Israel, and the people mourned greatly.*
>
> And they rose early in the morning and went up to the top of the mountain, saying, Here we are, and we will go up the place which the Lord has promised, for we have sinned!
>
> Then Moses said, Now why do you transgress the command of the Lord? For this will not succeed. Do not go up, lest ye be defeated by your enemies, *for the Lord is not among you.* for the Amalekites and the Canaanites are there before you, and you shall fall by the sword; because you have turned away from the Lord, *the Lord will not be with you.*" [Numbers 14:39-43 NKJ]

This is indeed a great tragedy. The power of the Lord which provided the covering for the people, supplying the basis for their invincibility, was facing away from where they were trying to go.

One vital lesson students learn in the school of faith, is that the power of the Lord, and the covering that it provides, is always in the direction of the commandment of the Lord to the individual or group. If they move away from that commandment of the Lord and the direction to which it is pointing them, they will automatically move away from its covering and protection, and consequently lose their invincibility. This may be why certain things happen in the lives of believers. An outsider may never be able to tell, because the answer is locked up in the records of that individual's personal walk with the Lord. The children of Israel learnt this lesson the hard way.

> "But they presumed to go up to the mountain top; nevertheless, neither the ark of the covenant of the Lord nor Moses departed from the camp.

> Then the Amalekites and the Canaanites who dwelt in that mountain came down and attacked them, and drove them back as far as Hormah." [Numbers 14:44-45 NKJ]

Moses would not be carried away by their emotional presumption which was out of touch and out of step with God. The result of such a presumption was predictably disastrous.

As students in the school of faith, these lessons are quite instructive to say the very least. But they have also posed certain questions about the duration of this school, and whether anybody does graduate out of it?

Chapter 10

INTEGRATING THE LESSONS OF THE SCHOOL OF FAITH

It would appear that what we have among the children of Israel and amongst Christians generally, are people who are at various grades or levels in the school of faith. An individual may move from Egypt through the wilderness, to Canaan the land of rest, in their walk before the Lord, but he or she never graduates from the school even in Canaan. Canaan affords him or her the opportunity to utilize the lessons learnt in the wilderness, harnessing the awesome powers of the Almighty God, to ensure his or her peace, progress, prosperity and blessings in the land of rest. But even in this, higher dimensions of lessons are revealed, and the student continues to grow wiser and wiser in the things of the Lord.

The Secret of Spiritual Strength

The apostle John had this to say to young men, who have proved themselves in the wilderness.

"...I have written unto you, young men, because you are strong, and the word of God abideth in you, and ye have overcome the wicked one." [1 John 2:14]

In this passage we have three factors that make for rest in Canaan, the promised haven of the believer, where faith in the Almighty God produces rest in the midst of mountains and giants of life.

I write to young men because, you are strong. In other words, you have strength in the inner man, spoken about in Ephesians 3:16.

"I pray that out of his glorious riches he may strengthen you with power through his Spirit in your inner being." [NIV]

This is Holy Ghost strength, that steadies the heart of man in any and every situation, imparting wisdom, guidance, and boldness to "take the bull by the horns." This is the power that prophet Micah wrote about in Micah chapter 3 verse 8, where he said:

"But truly *I am full of power by the Spirit of the Lord, and of justice and might,* to declare to Jacob his transgression and to Israel his sin." [NKJ]

This power enables a man or woman to stand up for God victoriously in every area of life, testifying eloquently to the victory in Christ and through Christ in every circumstance of life. It is tested and proven power.

John says to the young men, you are strong. I can see it. I have watched you in many situations, and I can say, yes, these guys are tough. They really know what they are doing.

The apostle outlined the secret of their strength. The secret is this: *The word of God abideth in you.* We immediately begin to see, that this strength being spoken of here is not macho strength, or bravado; not those who have learnt to bluff their way through many situations with little lies here and there for support. They are not those one may describe as "sneaky schemers" full of wiliness and guile. No. These are young men who know God through a deep and thorough study and assimilation of the nature of God, and the principles involved in walking with Him as revealed in the word of God, the Bible. These are men who have been through many stages in the Holy Spirit's *School of Discipleship,* from which nobody actually graduates on this side of eternity. The Holy Spirit has taught them the secret of following God through the experiences of various people outlined in both the Old and the New Testaments of the Bible, and they have been careful to learn and practice what they have been taught.

Again, these are men with combat experience, men who have been in action against the wicked one and his forces, and have tasted the sweet honey of victory. Here again is how he put it.

I write to you young men because....*you have overcome the wicked one.* What we learn here is that:

* Faith is no faith, until it has been tested and proven.

* Strength is no strength until it has been proven in battle against the enemy.

I write to you young men and women because you are strong. The way I know that you are strong is that I have seen you beat the devil hands down on several occasions. The devil has come against you with *fornication, adultery, lies, cheating, drug abuse, homosexuality, unbelief, idolatry, witchcraft, the lure of occult powers through transcendental meditation, through cults and secret societies; with the lure of demonic and satanic power through necromancy, oriental mysticism, idolatry, consorting with mediums and sorcerers.* I have seen the devil come against you in all sorts of ways, *lesbianism, anger, backbiting, gossip, envy, hatred, drunkenness, lust, pride, jealousy, self-pity, depression, grief, insecurity, oppression, persecution, slander, unemployment, retrenchment, bankruptcy threats and foreclosures, divorce, separation, sickness and disease, and all kinds of devices.* But on each occasion, I have watched you give the devil and his forces a technical knockout -TKO. Yes, I write to you young men and women because you are strong. Your secret is that the word of God abideth in you, because you entered and have remained in the Holy Spirit's school of discipleship, and He has taught you how to beat the devil and his crowd each time.

The Fruit of the Holy Spirit and the Spiritual Strength of the disciples

As the Holy Spirit is the only real teacher in the school of faith, the fruit He produces in the students becomes the bedrock of their defence against the fiery darts of the enemy. Let us see if we can capture the way it operates. The apostle John could easily have been saying to them: "Yes, I can see the strong cylindrical wall you have built around yourselves individually when you were in the school of faith, using the nine components of the *Fruit of the Holy Spirit* as bricks. I can see that each cross-section of your wall is nine blocks thick both vertically and horizontally, and you have so cleverly laid your brick that each of the component bricks shows up on the outside on the vertical plane at any cross-section. This has enabled you to face the devil with: *Love, Joy, Peace, Longsuffering, Kindness, Goodness, Faithfulness, Gentleness, Self-control* at one and the same time. The clever thing that you have done you strong young men and women, is that the devil and his folks have absolutely no clue what block is next in line at each cross-section.

The other day, I watched as the demon of lust attacked Brother Mark. The demon felt his *love* brick was a little bit confused, and so he couldn't quite say where love ended, for lust to begin. In fact he thought he was acting in love not knowing he was acting in lust. So, that part of his wall was breached. The demon then came against *kindness,* and that too was a bit confused, because Brother Mark was trying not to hurt anybody's feelings. There wasn't much of a resistance there. The demon was advancing, and Brother Mark was losing ground very fast. The next brick in line was *goodness.* There was some resistance there, because Brother Mark sensed he had broken the barrier between right and wrong. But that too, didn't last. That demon was lucky. It had really penetrated Brother Mark's defence. But then the next brick was *peace,* and there Brother Mark put up a spirited resistance because he had lost his peace completely. But as I watched the struggle I knew Brother Mark would soon win, for just behind *peace,* was *self-control.* That demon didn't know *self-control* was in there. He had cleverly avoided all the points on the external layer of bricks, where *self-control* was. As that demon hit *self-control,* it just lost power completely. Because unknown to the demon, Brother Mark had just charged up his *self-control* battery with a time of prayer and fasting. So when it was hit, it just fizzled out, and from *self-control* as the defence line, I saw brother Mark rebuild his *peace*, his *goodness*, his *kindness* and his *love*, in line with the mind of God as taught through the Bible in the Holy Spirit's school of discipleship.

I also watched Sister Grace's spirited fight against the combined forces of jealousy and envy. They had an easy access through *self-control* because as a very ambitious and dynamic person, Sister Grace breathed *self-control* as a success formula in life, long before she met the Lord. Besides, Sister Grace 'does not suffer fools gladly' or tolerate incompetence, and so she has not really charged up her *long-suffering or patience.* In fact she is known to say often that she has very little *patience* with people who are slow. Unfortunately for her on that line of defence, *long-suffering* was behind *self-control*, and it was beginning to look like a rout the way the two demons were penetrating. Her *joy,* and her *peace* went rather quickly too, because they too have not been developed much because of Sister Grace's impatience and ambitious drive to succeed. Sister Grace was truly in danger. It looked like all hope was lost. But unknown to the two demons, Sister Grace had just charged up her *love bricks* at a Holy Ghost seminar. But unfortunately for Sister Grace, *love* was the last brick on that defence line. The struggle dragged for a long time, as each brick offered as much resistance as it could before crumbling. The demons were elated at their success. Then they braced up for a finish. As they gathered up their strength and struck at her *love* brick, they were crushed to pieces instantly. For Sister Grace just went over and confessed her jealousy to Sister Mary and they both wept and prayed in repentance, and like a lightning, her *peace, longsuffering, joy, self-control etc.* were repaired.

This is why I write to you young men and women, because I know that you are indeed strong, and the word of God is staying right inside of you, and you knock out the devil and his folks all the time, Amen."

But it took quite a while for these young men and women to acquire these strengths. They entered the school of faith in the wilderness soon after the honeymoon.

The school of faith is a *sine qua non* or a must for every believer who wants to enjoy the rest that faith brings. For it is there that we learn about the various dimensions of faith, and so learn to respond to our circumstances with the right attitude, determined by our faith perception rather than our sight perception. This was the point the apostle Paul was making in 2nd Corinthians chapter 5, verse 7, where he said: *"For we walk by faith, not by sight."*

One thing we must note clearly is that, **God must first prove** (in the school of faith) **before He will bless**. When we go through the Scriptures, we are made to see that everyone who was blessed, was first proved. Three examples will suffice to illustrate this.

Abraham

This great man of God received a great promise from the Lord: *"In thee shall all the families of the earth be blessed"* Genesis 12 verse 3, when he had no child. He believed that promise and acted on it. Then, twenty-five years later, his wife Sarah had the long awaited son, Isaac. Abraham had seen the first reward of faith, and holding on to the very precious promises of God. But that was only a small portion of the package that the Almighty God had in store for him.

The question that God wanted to prove was: "Can anything or anyone force Abraham to re-order his priorities?" How else can this be proved, but through Abraham's most priceless possession, his son Isaac. God had earlier said of him: *"For I know him, that he will command his children and his household after him, and they shall keep the way of the Lord, to do justice and judgement; that the Lord may bring upon Abraham that which he hath spoken"* [Genesis 18:19 KJV] Can this commitment to follow and serve God still be upheld in any and every circumstance?

When Abraham passed the test in flying colours, (Genesis 22:1-19), God confirmed his blessings with these wonderful words:

"By myself have I sworn, saith the Lord, for because thou hast done this thing, and hast not withheld thy son, thine only son:

That in blessing I will bless thee, and in multiplying I will multiply thy seed as the stars of the heaven, and as the sand which is upon the sea shore; and thy seed shall possess the gates of his enemies; *And in thy Seed Shall All The Nations of The Earth be Blessed, Because Thou Hast Obeyed My Voice."* [Genesis 22:16-18]

There is a truth that is hidden here for all saints. As the sole teacher in the school of faith, the Holy Spirit is the one in charge of both the syllabus, and the examination. He decides when a candidate has had sufficient exposure to qualify for preliminary exams, and when a candidate is ready for the qualifying exam. Once a candidate has passed his or her qualifying exam in the school of faith, he or she will enter into his or her covenant blessing in the will of God for him or her, which is synonymous with the land of rest. The implication is that the individual can now be trusted to enter the promised land where there are mountains and giants, and find a wonderful place of rest there, dismissing the powers of giants and mountains so called, with the power of faith in the Almighty God. This is why failure to do this usually attracts the anger of God, for like the scriptures say: *"To whom much is given, much is required."* (Luke 12:48)

King Saul

King Saul's experience was a contrast to that of Abraham. He too went through the school of faith, but each time he went through the exams, he missed the grade that would have enabled him to enter into his own covenant blessing.

After Saul was crowned the first King of Israel, [1st Samuel 10:20-27] he passed his preliminary exams in the sense that he waited for the Lord to use an appropriate occasion to establish the kingdom in his hands. The war that the Ammonites planned against the city of Jabesh Gilead in Israel, [1st Samuel 11:1-15] provided the Lord the opportunity to make Israel rally behind Saul. But that was only the preliminary examination. Subsequent events were to prove that Saul had basic problems with respect to following God. He was spiritually naive. All these came out in under five years.

The Bible records that in the second year of Saul's reign, there was a war with the Philistines. This siege was such that some of the Hebrews ran across Jordan to escape what they considered a massacre. (1st Samuel 13 1-15) Saul and the prophet Samuel had a rendezvous at Gilgal, where Samuel was to offer prayers and sacrifices before the battle. The king arrived a week early and waited for the prophet. Unfortunately, the prophet was delayed. But more unfortunately, the king could not wait any longer, so he usurped the role of the prophet, an act that proved eternally disastrous. Many object lessons of the school of faith emerge as we look closely at that encounter between prophet and king. It offers tremendous lessons on what is, and what is not allowed in the walk of a man in faith before God.

> "And some of the Hebrews went over Jordan to the land of Gad and Gilead. As for Saul, he was yet in Gilgal, and all the people followed him trembling. And he tarried seven days, according to the set time that Samuel had appointed: but Samuel came not to Gilgal; and the people were scattered from him.
>
> And Saul said, Bring hither a burnt offering to me, and peace offerings. And he offered the burnt offering.
>
> And it came to pass, that as soon as he had made an end of offering the burnt offering, behold, Samuel came; and Saul went out to meet him, that he might salute him.
>
> And Samuel said, What hast thou done? And Saul said, Because I saw that the people were scattered from me, and that thou camest not within the days appointed, and that the Philistines gathered themselves at Mich'-mash;
>
> Therefore said I, The Philistines will come down now upon me to Gilgal, *and I have not made supplication unto the Lord*: I forced myself therefore, and offered a burnt offering.
>
> And Samuel said to Saul, *Thou hast done foolishly: Thou hast not kept the commandment of the Lord thy God, which He commanded thee: for now would the Lord have established thy kingdom upon Israel for ever*. But now thy kingdom shall not continue: the Lord hath sought him a man after his own heart, and the Lord hath commanded him to be captain over his people, *because thou hast*

not kept that which the Lord commanded thee." [1st Samuel 13:7-14 KJV]

Looking at this matter carefully, one may be inclined to say that Samuel's delay was responsible for this mortal sin of Saul. "Why on earth did he not keep the appointment." Saul analyzed his circumstances: the mass desertion of his troops, the multitude of his enemies on the siege, and then the delay of the prophet. "Since this supplication to the Lord was supposed to do the miracle that will discomfiture the Philistines, then let me as well do it. I can do it as well as the prophet, after all, I have watched him do it several times, and there is just nothing to it."

What he failed to realize was that a prophet is only a megaphone for the Almighty God. He cannot take one step without the approval of the Lord. From Samuel's rebuke of Saul, we realize that Saul, by that singular act, lost a significant part of his role in the history of the nation of Israel. This was the tragic judgement: *"--For now would the Lord have established thy kingdom upon Israel forever."* Samuel specifically said that he failed to keep the commandment of the Lord.

One could easily see the setting of that examination.

* "How long can Saul last in faith, in the presence of very intense pressure?

* Can he be depended on to trust the Lord absolutely even when the odds are heavily against him, or would he be tempted to compromise the commandments of the Lord."

No one knows now, how long this would have lasted. But what is quite revealing is that soon after his sin was completed, Samuel emerged.

The obvious lesson from the school of faith is that, an individual must wait on the Almighty God always, no matter how long it takes, and no matter what the pressures or circumstances may be. Later entrants to this school appear to have learnt this lesson from Saul's error.

> "Rest in the Lord, and *wait patiently* for him: fret not thyself because of him who prospereth in his way, because of the man who bringeth wicked devices to pass." [Psalm 37:7 KJV]

> "Trust in the Lord with all thine heart; and lean not unto thine own understanding. In all thy ways acknowledge him, and he shall direct thy paths. Be not wise in thine own eyes: fear the Lord and depart from evil." [Proverbs 3:5-7 KJV]

> "But they that wait upon the Lord shall renew their strength; they shall mount up with wings as eagles; they shall run and not be weary; and they shall walk, and not faint." [Isaiah 40:31 KJV]

> "For the vision is yet for an appointed time, but at the end it shall speak, and not lie: though it tarry, wait for it; because it will surely come, it will not tarry." [Habakkuk 2:3 KJV]

As we look at this very closely, a lesson that the Lord taught Samuel in the house of Jesse comes to mind immediately. "*---For the Lord does not see as man sees; for man looks at the outward appearance, but the Lord looks at the heart.*" [1st Samuel 16:7 NKJ]

It would appear that as a man goes through the school of faith, the Lord painstakingly notes, not just the things he or she says and does, but the thoughts of his hearts and his deepest yearnings, which may reflect a very deep reverence for, and commitment to God, or simply an opportunistic relationship designed to satisfy the needs of the individual. The latter will always invariably succumb to pressure, particularly prolonged pressure, while the former with its very stoic or stable disposition, will go to demonstrate the triumph of faith in God.

Those who in the depths of their hearts oscillate between the *desire to return to "Egypt,"* which typifies their old ways outside of God's kind of life, and *"Canaan,"* which typifies those who on their own have submitted their free will, intellect and emotions to the dictates of the theocentric or God-centred life, will always find in their lives' experiences, events similar to this Saul's experience. I call it *the tragedy of the prophet's "untimely arrival". Untimely, because it did result in sin, but timely enough to prove the individual's lack of dependability in the face of odds.*

This was the point Job was making to his friends, where he said: *"Though he slay me, yet will I trust in Him: but I will maintain my own ways before him. He also shall be my salvation: for an hypocrite shall not come before him."* [Job 13:15-16 KJV]

The prophet Habakkuk also captured this lesson which reflects the depth of commitment to the Lord.

> "Even though the fig trees are all destroyed, and there is neither blossom left nor fruit, and though the olive crops all fail, and the fields lie barren, even if the flocks die in the fields and the cattle barns are empty, yet I will rejoice in the Lord; I will be happy in the God of my salvation. The Lord God is my Strength, and he will give me the speed of a deer and bring me safely over the mountains." [Habakkuk 3:17-19 LB]

Students in the school of faith get to learn that the power of faith in the Almighty God, will always prevent such disasters as Habakkuk outlines above. But nevertheless they have steeled their innermost minds to such possibilities, and have already resolved that were such a possibility to emerge by default, it will in no way affect their loyalty to the Almighty God and His commandments.

In the matter of the destruction of the Amalekites recorded in 1st Samuel chapter 15, Saul again showed lack of progress in the school of faith. The problem was again the same, obeying the commandments of the Lord. Here is Samuel's damning indictment or accusation.

> "Hath the Lord as great delight in burnt offerings and sacrifices, as in obeying the voice of the Lord? Behold, *to obey is better than sacrifice, and to harken than the fat of rams.* For rebellion is as the sin of witchcraft, and stubbornness is as iniquity and idolatry. *because thou hast rejected the word of the Lord, He hath also rejected thee from being king.*" [1st Samuel 15:22,23 KJV]

One clear lesson from the record of King Saul's sojourn in the school of faith, is that a man must be careful to follow the instructions given to him by the Almighty God. This is the basis for the Lord's approval or disapproval of an individual. The king showed on two specific occasions, that he was incapable of doing this. But before we finish wondering whether these tests were not in fact too much too early, let us hasten to look at another student who came soon after Saul, King David.

King David

If we say that David must have learnt from the mistakes of Saul, it might not be too incorrect, as it was the same prophet Samuel, that crowned both of them. Although we are told that the coronation of David before his brethren as witnesses, was Samuel's last official act before his final retirement, it is not inconceivable to imagine that he must have warned David to carefully avoid the mortal mistakes of his immediate predecessor.

Anybody reading the Psalms will immediately see how David repeatedly admonished that we should wait patiently for the Lord, as in Psalm 37 verse 7. He knew what it was to wait patiently. His patience was sorely tested. As we look at the records, we notice how.

David was crowned king at the tender age of 20 years, when there was yet a king on his throne. What was he to do; contest for the throne with Saul? The answer was obviously no, a million times no. If anything, David carefully ensured that whatever will kill King Saul, will not be connected with him in any way.

He waited for the Lord to reveal him to Israel as the man to watch. In his encounter with Goliath of Philistia in 1st Samuel chapter 17, he was revealed to the whole of Israel as the man to come soon, just in the same way that the Lord used the threat to Jabesh Gilead by the Ammonites (1st Samuel 10) to reveal Saul to Israel as the man of the hour. As a result of this, his life was in danger at the hands of Saul. The king made several attempts to murder him. But in spite of all these, David made every effort to spare the life of the king. He had two clear opportunities to revenge, at the wilderness of Engeddi in 1st Samuel chapter 24, and in the wilderness of Zip in 1st Samuel chapter 26, but he restrained himself and his people, and indirectly chided Saul for his spiritual naivety.

> "And he said unto his men, The Lord forbid that I should do this thing unto my master, the Lord's anointed, to stretch forth mine hand against him, seeing he is the anointed of the Lord. So David stayed his servants with these words, and suffered them not to rise against Saul." [1st Samuel 24:6 KJV]

After they were parted from each other, he had these words for the king:

> "My lord the king-- Wherefore hearest thou men's words, saying, Behold, David seeketh thy hurt? Behold, this day thine eyes have seen how that the Lord had delivered thee to-day into mine hand in the cave: and some bade me kill thee: but mine eye spared thee; and I said, I will not put forth mine hand against my lord; for he is the Lord's anointed.-- The Lord judge between me and thee, and the Lord avenge me of thee: but mine hand shall not be upon thee." [1st Samuel 24:8,9,10, AND 12 KJV]

In this we may see how David was sorely tested of the Lord. Had he allowed his men to kill Saul, he would undoubtedly have precipitated a civil strife in Israel which may have cost him the throne in the end. But he had learnt in the school of faith, that a man may indeed be told by the Lord, the major role he is to play in life. But the matter of how, when and where, may be hidden from him. David had learnt that it is not for the individual to take matters into his own hands subsequently, and believing that God may be tardy or have forgotten, try to help Him along, often with disastrous consequences.

Even after it had been confirmed to David, that Saul was dead, he did not rush to grab the throne, rather he was careful to ascertain how the Lord planned to get him there.

> "In the course of time, David enquired of the Lord. "Shall I go up to one of the towns of Judah?" he asked. The Lord said, "Go up." David asked, "Where shall I go?" "To Hebron," the Lord answered.

So David went up there with his two wives, Ahinoam of Jezreel and Abigail, the widow of Nabal of Carmel. David also took the men who were with him, each with his family, and they settled in Hebron and its town. Then the men of Judah came to Hebron and there they anointed David king over the house of Judah."

First of all, the children of Judah his direct kinsmen made him their king. But Abner, Saul's Commander-in-Chief, took Saul's son Ish-Bosheth who was forty years old, and made him king over the rest of the house of Israel, and he reigned over them for two years. [2nd Samuel 2:8-10] David on the other hand reigned over the house of Judah alone for seven years and six months. All this time David was waiting for God's fullness of time. With time, Abner and his king, Ishbosheth both died, and the children of Israel then rallied round David, and anointed him king over the whole realm.

The sojourn of David in the school of faith as detailed in the Bible, also had its good scores and bad scores. His Achilles heel was the case of Bathsheba, the wife of Uriah the Hittite, [2nd Samuel chapters 12 and 13], and his secret ambition to embark on a global conquest as evidenced by the census he ordered in 2nd Samuel chapter 24.

But his deep love and reverence for the Almighty God, was manifested in his desire to build a temple for the Lord. [2nd Samuel chapter 7]. The depth of the Lord's pleasure at this is reflected in the personalized covenant, known today as the Davidic covenant, which he extracted from the Lord consequently.

"Now go and give this message to David from the Lord of heaven: I chose you to be the leader of my people Israel when you were a mere shepherd tending your sheep in the pasture land. I have been with you wherever you have gone and have destroyed your enemies. And I will make your name greater yet, so that you will be one of the most famous men in the world!---There will be no more wars against you; and your descendants shall rule this land for generations to come! For when you die, I will put one of your sons upon your throne and I will make his kingdom strong. He is the one who shall build me a temple. And I will continue his kingdom into eternity. I will be his father and he shall be my son. If he sins, I will use other nations to punish him, *but my love and kindness shall not leave him as I took it from saul,* your predecessor. *your family shall rule my kingdom forever."* [2nd Samuel 7:8,9, 11-16 LB]

What we are exposed to here is a crucial score in the school of faith, a mark awarded as a result of the eagerness of the student to outstrip his teacher's expectations. No wonder the Lord is quoted to have said of David: *"---I have found David the son of Jesse, a man after mine own heart, which shall fulfill all my will."* [Acts 13:22]

Summary of the School of Faith

The most fascinating thing about the school of faith is that most people who desire to walk with the Lord, are not conscious of the fact that they are in a school, where reviews, examinations and various kinds of performance tests are the order of the day. As a result of this, they do not make a conscious effort to walk before the Lord carefully, in the integrity of their heart.

We cannot gainsay the fact that the way an individual performs in the school of faith is what determines to a very large degree, the responsibilities that the Lord will entrust to him or her eventually.

When Peter declared in Acts chapter 10 verse 34, in the house of the Gentile convert Cornelius the centurion, that *God is no respecter of persons,* he was alluding to this performance of any and every individual in the school of faith. Said Peter;

"I now realise how true it is that God does not show favouritism but accepts men from every nation who fear Him and do what is right." [Acts 10:34-35 NIV]

Those in the school of faith, who consistently show insight into the ways of the Lord, are honoured by Him, and have the singular priviledge of enjoying a wonderful rest in Canaan, a land that flows with milk and honey, but which poses the inevitable challenges of mountains and giants as well as hostile neighbours. Learning to rest in the middle of all these, is proof of a good sojourn in the school of faith.

As we now stop to survey various dimensions of faith, we may find that we are in fact speaking of the various aspects of the lessons learnt in the Holy Spirit's school of faith.

Chapter 11

FAITH AS A SEED

In trying to appreciate the concept of faith as a seed, it is important to bear in mind that there are two basic aspects to it.

Faith as a seed will imply something that carries the potential within it for self regeneration. In other words, it has life within it. It also implies something that has the potential for growth. The fact that Jesus spoke in Matthew 17:20 about faith as a seed, choosing the mustard seed with its size and growth characteristics as His example, accentuates this fact. The mustard seed is singularly tiny, but the mustard tree by comparison is huge. So faith may be as tiny as the mustard seed, but if it is alive and active, then it has the capacity to grow into something big and significant. Implied here is the concept of the passage of time. In other words, it takes time for faith that is as tiny as a mustard seed, to become a mustard tree which can support so many things.

The difficulty we often have with respect to the development of faith, as well as its operation, stem from the fact that we ignore these factors of time and growth.

This is what is implied in Romans chapter 10 verse 17, where the Bible says: *"So then faith comes by hearing, and hearing by the word of God."*

Looking at this passage a little more closely, we may appreciate the concept of *dynamic* and *adynamic* states of the word of God heard by an individual. All a man may reflect in his life may be simply Bible knowledge. Bible knowledge is unfortunately not synonymous with faith. A learned Professor of Medicine once said that he had a distinction in high school in Bible knowledge, and so he knew it well enough not to want to read it again. Unfortunately, simple and pure Bible knowledge does not produce faith. Such knowledge will only constitute a quiescent seed, carrying the potential for life, but never coming alive all the same.

In order for faith to develop, the word must fuse with the Spirit to be ignited, galvanised or activated by the Life of God. Faith that comes through the word implies that the word on landing on the intellect of man, finds that part of his soul a watered ground, by which I mean, already sensitive to the life giving Spirit. The word then acquires life, becomes dynamic and begins to grow. The growth is dependent on the Spirit of God, who continuously infuses power into the word, transforming the individual's life and circumstance.

This was the point our Lord Jesus Christ was making to his disciples in John chapter 6, which was re-echoed by the Apostle Paul in his letter to the Corinthians.

> "It is the Spirit that quickeneth; the flesh [which we may rather call the intellect here] profiteth nothing: *the words that I speak unto you, they are Spirit, and they are life."* [John 6:63 KJV]

The apostle Paul went on to say further:

> "Not that we are competent in ourselves to claim anything for ourselves, but our competence comes from God. He has made us competent as ministers of a new covenant - *Not of the Letter* [which

in this case will represent mere adynamic words lacking power to transform life and its circumstances for the better] *But of the Spirit*; for the letter kills [produces frustrations and depressions] but the Spirit gives life." [2nd Corinthians 3:5&6 NIV]

It is because the word must be first activated by the Spirit of God, imparting the revelation knowledge in the word to the heart of the individual, and causing it to grip the mind with the power derived from the Spirit of God, that the individual requires consistent meditation to progressively build up his faith. An individual may merely read and acquire head knowledge. What faith needs to grow is *revelation knowledge*, which exposes the power in the word. When Jesus said; " *the words I speak to you are spirit and life"*, He was referring to this transforming power inherent in the word that has been quickened by the Spirit of God.

An individual who consistently meditates on the word of God, is like someone providing raw materials for a factory. The raw materials may be used immediately for processing end products, or they may be reserved for a more auspicious moment.

When we speak of the dimensions of faith, we refer to the individual who runs a multi-purpose factory, and has stored up several kinds of raw materials required to produce different kinds of products. Since he is not sure what the customer will require, he prepares to produce whatsoever the demand is. He has the *"Faith Answer"* for every demand of the world and the devil.

The concept of faith as a seed therefore reflects this painstaking effort the individual makes daily to equip himself or herself with the raw materials of the word of God, enabling the Holy Spirit of God to build him or her up solidly in any and all directions, making his or her life impenetrable to any dart of the enemy.

This is the very point the apostle Paul was making in Ephesians chapter 6, verse 16 where he said:

"In addition to all these, *take on the shield of faith*, with which you can extinguish all the flaming arrows of the evil one". [NIV]

The truth is that the evil one does not just shoot one kind of arrow, neither does he shoot them in only one direction. We know that what is true to life is that people have to learn how to deal with all kinds of situations. Some of these situations just come and go; others come and would wish to stay and some of these do hang around for a little while before we finally figure out how to get rid of them. Some come head on, from the office, workshop or neighbours; others creep in from unexpected quarters like home, church and fellowship.

But no matter when they come, how long they have been around or where they are coming from, faith always has an answer for every situation. Faith does not confront all situations the same way. It has various dimensions it uses to attack different situations depending on their attributes, in order to successfully quench their flaming arrows.

It is our failure to recognize this that causes many an individual to sometimes go to the preacher and say: "My faith isn't working any more. It had always worked until now. I just do not seem to figure out what is going on any more. Please kindly lay your hands on me and pray for me."

The solution to a situation like this may lie in the dimensions of faith, and we may proceed to look at some dimensions now.

Chapter 12

FULFILLING OUR OBEDIENCE OF CHRIST

The apostle Paul, by the Holy Spirit, writing to the church at Corinth, informed them that there is a way an individual can avenge all disobedience of Christ in his or her life. It was like saying to them: *"Hey, you folks can teach the devil a good lesson anytime he tries to mess around with you. But you've got to know that you just can't do it any way. There is a way you can do it, and here is it:"*

> "For though we walk in the flesh, we do not war after the flesh: (For the weapons of our warfare are not carnal, but mighty through God to the pulling down of strongholds;) Casting down imaginations, and every high thing that exalteth itself against the knowledge of God, and bringing into captivity every thought to the obedience of Christ;
>
> And having in a readiness to revenge all disobedience, *when your obedience is fulfilled."* [2nd Corinthians 10:3-6 KJV]

The implication of this passage is that anybody who wants to avenge all disobedience of Christ in his life, be it his physical, spiritual, emotional or material life, has got to make sure that he has done all the things that the good Lord has revealed to his heart with respect to that issue.

I believe this is where many of us miss the point a great many times. We seem to have dissociated our obedience of the things the Lord has revealed to us in a particular situation, from our ability to exercise the power and authority in Christ at work in us, in those circumstances in particular. Even in ordinary life, anybody can see the hypocrisy inherent in that. It is often reflected in a question like this: "What moral right do you have to command me, when you have not obeyed a single thing you have been told on this matter?"

The truth is that the individual may indeed command, and command and command interminably, but the power to effect the desired change will not come down, because the circuit has not been completed. The power will come down when our obedience is fulfilled.

There is a song we sing that reflects the essence of this thought. The first two lines go like this:

The Lord knows the way through the wilderness
All I have to do is to follow

The implication of this is that the things the Lord is urging me to do will lead me out of my dilemma if I am careful to follow His instructions that I have understood properly. There is no particular safe haven implied when I qualify the Lord's instructions as those I have understood properly, because often times the problem is not that I have not understood the instructions, the problem is that they are not convenient.

It is like the case of the proverbial lady who was advised by the preacher that the solution to her problem at home lies in her ability to submit to her husband as the head of the home, who turned round and said rather defensively: "Well Sir, it is because you do not know my husband, that is why you can suggest a thing like that."

In one vein we earnestly desire the Lord to intervene in our circumstances as we exercise our faith in Him. In another vein we refuse to obey the things He has written with respect to those very issues.

A gentleman who, confronted with this kind of reality had to pray: *"Lord, bless me anyway."* The truth is that such anyway prayers do not go anywhere. They often represent mere wishful thinking.

When we stop to analyze this fully, we find that what is at the bottom line is, *the cardinal place of the will of God in the life of the individual Christian*.

Anyone who dares to ignore this in his or her walk with God, is bound to meet with frustrations incessantly. Sometimes, even the circumstances we are praying about in themselves are by-products of our failure to walk in the will of God in the first place.

Determining the will of God in a particular situation, and going ahead to walk in that will is the *foundational dimension of faith*. The individual will be fulfilling all his or her known "obedience," thereby making himself or herself ready to avenge all disobedience of Christ.

One may wonder whether there is any distinction between walking in the will of God, and asking according to His will which the apostle John wrote about in his first epistle to the church.

> "And this is the confidence that we have in him, that, if we ask anything according to his will, he heareth us: And if we know that he hear us, whatsoever we ask, we know that we have the petitions that we desired of him." [1 John 5:14,15 KJV]

Indeed there is a distinction. For when we speak of walking in the will of God, we are referring to the various principles and commands that are revealed in the word of God, the Bible, as well as the personal instructions given to us by the Holy Spirit through some kind of revelation, either directly to us in our hearts, or through other vessels, but confirmed in us by what is commonly referred to as, *"the inward witness."* On the other hand, when we speak of asking according to the will of God, we are referring to our awareness of the promises already made by the Lord with respect to those needs as revealed in His word, and structuring our prayers in line with the contents of such promises. What the apostle John is saying is that when we structure our prayers according to His promises, we are guaranteed answers to those prayers.

One may then wonder, would a conflict not arise sooner than later? All we need to answer a question like that is to just look up any promise in the word of God, and we would discover that behind each promise is some controlling principle to be followed. Take the oft quoted promise in Philippians chapter 4, verse 19:

"But my God shall supply all your need according to his riches in glory by Christ Jesus." [KJV]

A man may read this and shout: "Thank God for a blank cheque. I can fill in any amount of money I want."

A blank cheque indeed it is, but made out to who? That is where the problem is. Its good to make sure you have your name on one of those blank cheque leaves, or you might end up in trouble if you present them to the bank of heaven to make it good. Verses 15 to 18 of the same chapter, tell us something about those qualified to go ahead and cash that cheque.

> "As you well know, when I first brought the Gospel to you and then went on my way, leaving Macedonia, only you Philippians became my partners in giving and receiving. No other church did this. Even when I was over in Thessalonica you sent help twice. But though I appreciate your gifts, what makes me happiest is the well earned reward you will have because of your kindness.
>
> At the moment I have all I need - more than I need! I am generously supplied with the gifts you sent me when Epaphroditus came. They are a sweet smelling sacrifice that pleases God well." [LB]

What is obvious in the four verses preceding verse 19, is that the promise was made to very willing partners in the spread of the Gospel of our Lord and Saviour Jesus Christ. These partners became partners on their own initiative, and were in fact the first ones in all the churches to do this. An individual may have some of his or her needs supplied one way or the other. But this promise to supply all needs was made to those who were willing partners in the spread of the Gospel. The reason is not too difficult to find.

> "For God, who gives seed to the farmer to plant, and later on, good crops to harvest and eat, will give you more and more seed to plant and will make it grow so that you can give away more and more fruit from your harvest. Yes, *God will give you much so you can give away much*, and when we take your gifts to those who need them *they will break out into thanksgiving and praise to God for your help.*" [2nd Corinthians 9:10,11 LB]

One can multiply this example in the word of God. Ignoring the vital principles behind the promises, undercuts the supply of the Holy Ghost power required to meet the needs.

As we walk by faith before the Lord, we must always put the factor of His will in every situation in constant perspective. If we are able to do this, then we would have laid a very solid foundation for a continuing answer to all our prayer needs.

Chapter 13

INGREDIENTS OF CREATIVE FAITH

When most people talk about faith, this is really what they mean. An individual hears the word of God, receives it into his heart as the living word of the Almighty God, and so believes it with all his heart. Because he believes that the power of God is right behind His word, he goes ahead to confess the word as reality. As he confesses the word, it acquires creative potential through the omnipotence of God, and so he proceeds to receive that which he heard and believed with his heart, and which by confession he has caused to be by the power of God.

Our Lord Jesus used the incidence of the fig tree recorded in Mark chapter 11 to teach this vital lesson. The story as told by Mark in his gospel account is quite revealing. Jesus was hungry. He saw a fig tree and thought he could get something out of it. The fig tree had nothing to offer. Jesus said to the tree: *"Let no one eat fruit from you ever again."* His disciples were there and heard this rather strange exchange. They thought nothing of it at the time. The next day however, Peter was shocked to observe that the tree had actually died.

This is where the lesson on this dimension of faith actually begins, when we start to throw away old ideas. As far as the disciples were concerned, it was just a strange exchange. They never for one moment thought that anything this dramatic could result from such an exchange. This is why Peter said: *"Rabbi, look! The fig tree which You cursed has withered away."*

It is not that difficult to explain the reason behind Peter's surprise. He never expected any such thing to happen to the fig tree. Jesus spoke the words. His hearers did not believe what He said, and because they did not believe it, they had no expectations that what He said would actually come to pass so quickly. Besides, what connection is there between mere words, and hard core reality.

Jesus took the opportunity thus created, to teach a vital lesson on faith. He said to the people:

> "Have faith in God. For assuredly, I say to you, whoever says to this mountain, Be removed and be cast into the sea, and does not doubt in his heart, but believes that those things he says will come to pass, *he will have whatever he says.*
>
> Therefore I say to you, whatever things you ask when you pray, believe that you receive them, and you will have them" [Mark 11:22-24 NKJ]

Commentators have told us that what Jesus said was more like, *"Have faith like God."* That certainly would explain the vital lessons that followed. Jesus was in other words saying to the people: "This is the way God operates. If you say something, and believe that what you have said will come to pass without wavering in your mind, what you said will indeed come to pass." We may simply say that Jesus was teaching the vital ingredients of *creative faith,* which are, *Believing, Confessing, Expecting,* and *Receiving.* We may stop to examine each one of them in some detail.

Believing

How does one get to believe the word of God to the extent that what he has believed acquires creative potential?

The apostle Paul says in Romans chapter 10, that they must first hear the word of God and understand it through the help of a preacher or teacher. This teacher of course will always be a representative of the Teacher, the Holy Spirit of God, (John 14:26) who may choose to either do it through an instrument or do it directly Himself.

> "How then shall they call on Him in whom they have not believed? And how shall they believe in Him of whom they have not heard? And how shall they hear without a preacher?
>
> So then faith comes by hearing, and hearing by the word of God." [Romans 10:14, 17 NKJ]

An individual may therefore hear the word of God either by reading it himself and allowing the Holy Spirit of God to explain it to his heart, and assist his understanding to grasp the true meaning of what has been written down for us, or he may have it explained to him by the same Holy Spirit but this time using the preacher or the evangelist as the instrument.

But mere hearing will not constitute faith or believing except the mind or the intellect grasps the true essence of the word that he has heard. The mind must grasp its meaning, implication and application with respect to God and man.

This will still not constitute faith by itself. For having understood the word, its implications and applications, the individual must now cast off his previous parallel beliefs, and replace them with the new thing he has learnt. This will ensure that when he rests his confidence on the new truth that he has learnt, it will be an exclusive support, his parallel and counter beliefs having been allowed to wither and drop off like the shrivelled fig tree above.

Oftentimes, this is where problems begin to arise. I once heard the story of a man who was hanging on a rope in a canyon, between heaven and earth as it were. He called out desperately for help, and a deep voice responded: *"I am God, I have come to help you. Let go of the rope you are holding on to, and I will help you."* The gentleman then called out: *"Is there anyone else out there?"*

Believing must involve casting off previous supports and notions that have failed to meet our needs in the past. It must also include concepts and ideas that we have imbibed over time in various circles and settings which are opposed to the revealed mind of God in His word. *Old crutches must be dropped for faith to thrive unhindered.*

It is possible for one to get this far, and still find that faith has not begun to operate. The reason is because creative faith is a spiritual phenomenon that represents the moment of transcription, when the written word becomes the living word by acquiring the anointing, or Holy Ghost momentum, in the heart of the individual. Once that happens, *the individual will know, that he knows, that he knows, that he knows, ad infinitum*, that God has answered. The assurance almost acquires tangibility. Doubt is completely swallowed up in the face of the imminent reality created by faith.

Sometimes this will follow the moment the individual understands the word of God, its implications and applications. Some other times it will not. Where it does not, then believing must be followed immediately by *Confessing* and *Expecting* the object of our faith.

Confessing and Expecting the Object of our Faith

This is crucial to the development of creative faith. Like we said before, it is not always that this is necessary, for the grace of God ensures that most things come to us through His loving anticipation of our needs operating through His foreknowledge. That is why Jesus said we should speak few words when we pray, since the Father already knows what we need. [Matthew 6:8]

What confessing and expecting the object of our faith as revealed in God's word do therefore, is to *help propel the knowledge of God's word stored in the intellect to the Spirit, assisting it thereby to acquire Holy Ghost momentum.* In other words, through confessing and expecting we keep what we believe at the top of our minds so that the next time a wave of Holy Ghost anointing passes by us as it were, it will impart creative potential to our faith. When our faith is thus activated, then we know, that we know, that we know that our answer is right at the door. The impact of the Holy Spirit on faith sustained through confession and expectation may be described as some kind of *activation.*

Besides by *confessing* and *expecting,* we simply crowd out doubt, filling the mind with the expected reality. Also, the desires of our hearts and the words we speak are brought together in an agreement, discharging the same spiritual signals heavenward to the throne room of the Almighty God.

This was the point that our Lord Jesus Christ was making when he was teaching on the incidence of the withered fig tree. What you believe in your heart, which you keep saying with your mouth, will undoubtedly come to pass in your experience much sooner than you can imagine by the same power that the Almighty God uses to effect His will in the universe.

I recall the testimony of a lady who had been married for three years without any issue. She had longed for a baby of her own, and had believed God with all her heart. As we all know, a problem like this has a monthly cycle, and one has to wait for the menstrual period to come and pass at the end of the cycle to know whether conception had resulted.

She confessed that she used to be so upset each time she saw her period, and would go to God complaining bitterly about being disappointed.

She would however seek no other powers. She visited her obstetrician and had routine investigations done, and was told that things were normal biologically.

This ding-dong affair however continued for three whole years, with the lady getting angrier and angrier at God, and more and more frustrated. Then one day she knelt down and poured out her heart in confession to God. She said an unusual thing happened to her after that prayer. She got off her knees with a stunning conviction that she would have her baby. At the end of that monthly cycle, she still had her period as usual; but this time around, rather than become angry, she started to confess that the devil was a liar, and that her baby was on the way. The next monthly cycle still saw her period. She decided it was really time to now praise the Lord for her baby. Gone were all the bitterness and all the anger. The third cycle saw the baby on the way, and she has had four children since then.

Receiving the Object of our faith

This is the predictable end of the road for faith that has been processed in this way. Our expectation of it hastens it to us, as it were, driven by the power of God which was working through our faith in His written or spoken word.

Creative Faith and the Spoken word

For purposes of clarity, we may like to distinguish the confession of our faith, which is the word of God that we have believed in our hearts, from the spoken word which is the mind of God as revealed to us.

An example will help to illustrate this. Suppose I desire to own a house of my own today. I may go to God in prayer, and believe Him for it. I may use as my faith anchor any scripture that is appropriate which the Holy Spirit brings to my mind. Let us take a Scripture like: *"Delight yourself also in the Lord, And He shall give you the desires of your heart"* [Psalm 37:4] Since there is a condition to that promise I would try to check whether indeed I have delighted myself in my God. Having satisfied myself that I have, I would then proceed to believe God for this and start to claim it until it materializes, however long that may take.

But suppose the Lord were to say to me by revelation: *"Son, I will cause you to own your own house by this time next year."* It is obvious that the two are quite different. What I have in the previous one is the desire of my heart which I have presented before my God. On the other hand, the second example is the mind of God concerning my life revealed to me in time.

I have a friend whose wife had three children all of whom were girls. He was an only boy in his family, and naturally he desired to have at least one male child to complement his girls. His wife wanted it very much and prayed to the Lord for it. They were such fine Christians, everyone admired them.

One morning she called at my home rather early for some medical consultation, and I noticed the heaviness in her heart. As soon as she departed, I went into my closet and said to the Lord: "Dear Lord, please give this lady the desires of her heart." Suddenly the Lord started to speak to me. He told me to let her know that she would have a baby boy in nine months. She did.

There is a key principle that operates, when the mind of God about any particular issue is revealed in time. The apostle Paul captured this in his letter to the Romans, chapter 4, verse 17 where he talked about God who gives life to the dead and *calls those things which do not exist as though they did.*

For an individual to begin to call forth those things that do not exist as though they did, *what is being called forth must specifically be in the will of God as revealed in time.* It is not enough for it to be in the general form of the will of God for believers. For this to operate effectively, what is being called forth must be in the will of God for that individual at that particular time, as revealed to that individual by the Lord.

If God says: *"Son, by this time next year, I shall cause you to own your own house",* I can begin from then on to call forth my house knowing that God has moved that blessing into the orbit of time.

To begin to call forth something that has not been willed in time by the Lord may lead to a lot of frustration for the individual. This is because there would be no result. But once the mind of the Lord has been revealed, then one can begin to "call forth those things that be not as though they were".

Those who ignore these principles create an opportunity for the enemy to put a wedge in their relationship with their Father in heaven.

When a man is confessing and expecting an object of faith, his faith is progressively being built up. But when a man is calling forth, he is acting like the Lord did on creation morning, when He called forth the world He had willed in His heart, into existence.

I have met quite a number of people during counselling, who have had some problems in this area. Often times, the problem arose because there was someone somewhere, who successfully called his or her need into existence. As a result of this, they then resort to calling forth their own needs into existence as well, expecting the same results. Historical accounts of other peoples' experiences undoubtedly serve to encourage us in our faith. The truth however is that most of the time, the stories are started halfway where they are interesting. All the struggles that brought the individuals to that state are left untold, because sometimes they tended to reduce what they have judged to be the impact of the accounts. The result is that people only here about the "*birth*," but not about how Zion travailed to bring it to pass. [Isaiah 66:8]

But wherever and whenever conditions are right, the result is always similar, for the Bible has already told us that God is no respecter of persons. [Acts 10:34}

It is important to grasp the distinction between these two, for this in part is the whole purpose of this book, *faith dimensions*. When an individual is face to face with a situation, he should be able to determine how best to approach the matter. In other words, what dimension of faith is best suited for this situation. Or better still, what faith strategy can I apply in order to move my need from eternity to time, where I require it to solve some problems in my life?

To insist that faith operates in only one dimension, which a brother has classified as *'name it and claim it,'* is to court frustration and by implication a stuttering Christian life experience.

All of life situations are not amenable to one dimension of faith. Several dimensions are taught in the word of God, and it behoves us in our own interest to become familiar with all these dimensions, and selectively apply the one that is most appropriate in a given situation.

Chapter 14

PATIENCE

This dimension of faith operates very closely with creative faith commonly known as *believing, confessing, expecting* and *receiving*. It has a great deal to do with the period of expectation.

In the book of Hebrews chapter 10, verses 35 and 36, we are told:

> "Cast not away therefore your confidence, which hath great recompense of reward. For you have need of patience, that, after you have done the will of God, ye might receive the promise." [KJV]

The new King James Version says:

> "You have need of endurance, so that after you have done the will of God, you may receive the promise"

It was Richard Rich in *"A Man for all Seasons"* by Robert Bolt, who said to Thomas Moore: " Waiting is work." Indeed waiting can play some funny tricks on the balance of mind of an individual. But the apostle James counsels that we should let patience have its perfect work, said he in James chapter 1, verse 4:

> "But let patience have its perfect work, that you may be perfect and complete, lacking nothing."

This is the way the Living Bible puts it:

> "For when the way is rough, your patience has a chance to grow. So let it grow, and don't try to squirm out of your problems. For

when your patience is finally in full bloom, then you will be ready for anything, strong in character, full and complete."

It is this maturing effect of patience that comes into play once the answer to a need is delayed.

Yet this patience is in fact a dimension of faith. While we are confessing and expecting, time may begin to wear down our resolve, and circumstances may begin to compel us to despair and sometimes accuse God of being indifferent to our situation. We can capture this sentiment in the words of the Psalmist where he said:

> "Awake! Why do You sleep, O Lord? Arise! Do not cast us off forever. Why do You hide Your face, And forget our affliction?
>
> For our soul is bowed down to the dust; Our body clings to the ground. Arise for our help, And redeem us for Your mercies' sake." [Psalm 44:23-26 NKJ]

An individual that is compelled to wait, may wait in quiet assurance as taught in the Holy Spirit's school of faith, confident that the Lord will come at the fullness of time. This kind of waiting brings out the fine distinction between *faith* and *hope.*

When we wait in hope, expectation is quite low because of the indefiniteness of hope. In fact sometimes, expectation is completely non-existent. Hope is interminable. But hope is non-the-less a sustaining concept, that builds a great degree of perseverance into us. God will come one day, some day. But He will certainly come nevertheless.

There are some things we can only hope for. They are usually things that are totally outside our control which are in the future, like the hope of eternal life. The apostle Paul said of that; *"If in this life only we have hope in Christ, we are of all men most pitiable."* Hope in this regard is born of faith in the fact that the Almighty God being unchanging by nature, (Malachi 3:6), will keep His word to all those who have run for refuge in the covenant relationship in Jesus Christ.

When we wait in faith however, there is an element of dynamism that sustains expectation. What we are believing the Lord for, we are expecting in time, some definite time in our experience. Our confession is that God will come and He will not tarry. In other words He will not be half a second late. Waiting in faith is therefore waiting with a sustained expectation, sustained by the attributes of God we have learnt and experienced in the school of faith in the wilderness. Several Bible writers also captured this thought. The prophet Habakkuk had this to say as stated earlier:

> "For the vision is yet for an appointed time; but at the end it will speak, and it will not lie. *though it tarries, wait for it; because it will surely come, it will not tarry."*

I have heard several people express this thought in prayer like this: "Dear Lord, we know that delay is not denial..."

The responsibility we have is to ensure that we are waiting in faith rather than in hope. Confession and expectation will ensure for us that the issue is in perspective in line with the promises of God on the matter.

It will be quite frivolous to suggest that this pathway here outlined is an easy road to walk. Patience is indeed a virtue, and a great one at that. In Galatians 5:22 it is listed as one of the components of the fruit which the indwelling Holy Spirit bears in the life of the believer.

Those who have learnt to walk closely with the Holy Spirit on a daily basis will experience how He encourages patience in us through communion by constantly reminding us of the promises of the Lord in general, with respect to the issue, and in the particular situation we are in as He has revealed it to our hearts. But patience as a dimension of faith does not stand in isolation. It is complemented by others which are equally of vital importance to our spiritual and overall health and stability.

Chapter 15

PRAISE AND THANKSGIVING

Merlin Carothers of Prison to Praise fame can be described as the modern day great exponent of the Praise dimension of faith.

I recall that on more than one occasion we had sat down in the executive meeting of the Full Gospel Business Men's Fellowship International, FGBMFI, Ikeja Chapter here in Lagos, Nigeria, to dissect the fine distinctions between 1st Thessalonians chapter 5, verse 18, and Ephesians 4:20. Here is what they say:

> "In everything give thanks; for this is the will of God in Christ Jesus for you." [1st Thessalonians 5:18 NKJ]

> "Giving thanks always for all things to God the Father in the name of our Lord Jesus Christ." [Ephesians 5:20 NKJ]

The crux of the matter lies in the distinction between; *for everything...and, in everything.* There was a general agreement on each occasion that it is not too difficult to see how one can give thanks in every situation, whatever that situation may be. You can always find some space in God's omnipotence, Omnipresence and Omniscience to bury any and every situation however difficult or unpleasant. One can always say: "this may be a surprise to me, but it certainly is not a surprise to God. I may not be able to do anything about this, but God certainly can. I may not have been were this decision was taken, but God was certainly there. It therefore remains for me to seek out the purpose or purposes of the Lord in all this so that I can maximally benefit from the experience."

When it comes to giving thanks for every situation, there is an understandable dilemma. For example should I praise God for my smashed automobile, dead brother or sister, collapsed investment or retrenchment? How can an individual in his right senses do something like that?

A veteran may simply say, *"yea! you surely can. You may not feel it, but just go ahead and do it anyway."*

Sometimes, when you try to do it this way the veteran has said, you feel a great sense of revulsion. You feel there is something hypocritical about doing it. In other words, you find that you cannot do it in faith.

Grappling with this thought has provided a lot of relief for me in the past as the Lord shed light on what is hereby implied.

Indeed, the mind may have understandable difficulties giving thanks for all things particularly in the middle of a great deal of heartache or pain.

There is nothing to thank God for in pain, disaster, retrenchment, death, foreclosure and the like events, by themselves. Indeed there is nothing. But one can thank God *for what He is going to do in these situations*. The thanksgiving is therefore not for the situations per se, but *for what God is going to do through them to bring glory and honour to His name.*

It is what God will do in the midst of these situations that will turn an apparent defeat into a major victory, and provide a basis for faith and praise.

Faith reaches beyond the prevailing situation to praise God for what is soon to be, which will destroy the impact of the particular event in our lives.

When the preacher says: "My dear, you may not feel like it, but praise the Lord anyway," a deeply hurt individual may feel that the preacher is devoid of understanding and cannot empathise for lack of experience. Indeed the preacher may not have sat where you are sitting at that particular moment, but since Jesus has, we can praise Him for what He will do to glorify His name through the very unpleasant situation.

As a dimension of faith, praise and thanksgiving provides a great deal of inner healing, releasing our soul to begin to exercise faith again. They are ready cures for depression in times of distress, if the mind can be lifted away from the situation, on to what the Almighty God is about to unfold through it all.

One thought that is very helpful is realising that we are citizens of heaven passing through the earth. Each experience we undergo in Christ is designed to produce the finest in us. For example, an adverse situation may provide an impetus to dig deeply on the authority of the believer, so that we can learn how to stop the devil in our lives. The adverse situation itself may have been brought about by our complacence, and laziness, as well as our lack of spiritual development despite years of tutelage.

What is hereby implied is a positive attitude to every situation however adverse. Focusing on what God is about to unfold in an adverse situation removes the sting out of it, and as it were robs the enemy of his glee. Besides, it ensures for us that we are open to discover the way of escape in every situation promised by the Lord in 1st Corinthians 10:13

So when we praise God for the situation, we are praising Him for the progress we are making and are going to make heavenward, which will in turn make our journey here on earth smoother and more enjoyable.

Praise and thanksgiving are also necessary appendages of confessing and expecting the object of our faith. It is a way we say to God rather eloquently: *"Dear Lord, I have filed this request away because I know that You have noted it. I thank You because You have already sent it, and I will soon receive it."* Having said that our confession and expectation change to praise, thanksgiving and expectation.

It is in this sense that praise is regarded as one of the highest forms of prayer because they express our confidence in God in the way the Lord deeply appreciates. This is why He said: *"He that offereth praise, glorifieth me."* [Psalm 50:23 KJV].

But there are yet other dimensions of faith.

Chapter 16

THE SEED MUST DIE

Part of the search that gave birth to this book derived from some of my own personal frustrations with respect to meeting my needs under God. At a stage in one's life as a Christian, you tend to come away with the impression that you now have a grasp or at least some idea of what it means to walk with the Lord in faith. Then all of a sudden something happens, and you begin to apply all that you have learnt over the years, and nothing seems to work. Nothing that you had known up till that moment appears to hold the key to the problem. You have believed, sought the will of God, confessed, expected and praised, and yet nothing seems to move the problem. Then all of a sudden you remember patience, and you decide to wait in fasting and prayer, believing, confessing, expecting for as long as you possibly can. Still nothing happens. So what on earth is the matter. What can hold the key to this problem?

As I look around me today, I can count quite a number of people that I know who are also wondering what next to do. They have just about done anything and everything they know how to do, and the problem still persists as it were.

As I meditated on this subject years ago, I discovered that faith has yet this dimension, which I have chosen to call, *The Seed Must Die to Live*. This concept derives from John chapter 12, verse 24.

"Most assuredly, I say to you, unless a grain of wheat falls into the ground and dies, it remains alone; but if it dies, it produces much grain." [NKJ]

Sometimes we are faced in our lives with certain situations that will not go away. The problem is not just that these situations will not go away, but that they cause us a great deal of heartache and frustration, and often create great bitterness and anger in our hearts.

Most of the time it did not start that way. We started the normal way believing that our answer would overtake us much sooner than later. But as days become weeks, and weeks become months, and months become years, our frustration grows into anger, then depression, and sometimes total disillusionment. It is not everyone that has the capacity to live down situations like this. Some people in fact, end up giving up their faith totally.

A couple of months ago, I met a desperate young lady who was angered by the fact that all her suitors were people she considered unmarriageable, despite all her prayers and dedication to God. Another young lady threw her faith out the window because according to her, God could not solve a simple examination problem. She had failed repeatedly.

I doubt that there is any Christian who has not come face to face with difficult situations in his or her life, which tended to persist.

The concept of life through death as a dimension of faith shines forth gloriously in circumstances like these. The truth is that so long as we are angry, frustrated, bitter, depressed and disenchanted, we cannot exercise faith. All that we present each time we come to the throne of grace is a catalogue of complaints that reflect our disappointment and frustration with the way things are going with us. Under such circumstances, it is impossible to hear what God is saying clearly, since we are pre-occupied with what we think He should be saying and doing.

Being able to die to that need is a great dimension of faith, which brings inner healing and releases our soul and our spirit to soar in faith to God again. The apostle Paul declares in Romans chapter 6, verse 7:

"For he who has died has been freed from sin." [NKJ]

This speaks about releasing ourselves from the pressure, the tremendous psychological and emotional pressures inherent in the pursuit of that need, which had built up over time. Until we die to that need, those pressures will not cease, and so long as those pressures persist, being able to hear the Lord clearly on the matter will remain a significant obstacle to the attainment of the objective.

In plainer language, we may say rather categorically, and without any fear of contradiction that certain needs in the life of the individual will not be met except he or she dies to them. The reason is that those needs have become rather overbearing, constituting themselves into a consuming passion, an obsession in fact, which has totally paralysed our waking thoughts. Given that kind of scenario, God's relevance to the individual, is secretly being judged by how He is responding to that need.

The only way to break away from this cycle of spiritual death is to die to that need. One can die to a need if he can look at that need squarely, with all that it means to him, and say to God: "Lord, you know how much I desire to have this thing. You know what it means to me. You know how angry it has made me all these years. You know how it has created a wedge in our communion several times. I am sorry for all those anger, bitterness, murmuring and complaints; all those expressions of frustration and disillusionment. I ask you to please forgive me now Lord. But before I stop Lord, I would like to say one thing more. I am leaving this matter now in Your hand for the very last time. If You want it for me, then I want it. If You do not want it for me, then I do not want it, and there, is where I have chosen to end it. Thank You for restoring my peace. *I die to this need once and for all.* By Your grace, I am free, totally free from its crushing oppression. Thank You for Your victory in me, in Jesus name, Amen."

Being able to die to a need produces inner healing and restores faith. The individual is able once again to relate with God, without having an issue loom so high in his or her consciousness that it obstructs the person's relationship with God.

This is one sure way of identifying issues that call for life through death. They are usually those things that have converted themselves into an obsession.

Take the issue of a husband or wife, praying for their spouse's conversion to Christ. They begin by witnessing to them, and inviting them to several kinds of meetings, and out-reaches. Each time an altar call is made for people to receive Christ, they reach out to God agonizingly. But as days progress to weeks, weeks to months, and months to years, and nothing seems to happen, they become frustrated, irritable and quarrelsome at home. They are angry with God during their prayers, and even at home, they forget in their depression to be exemplary Christians in order to encourage their spouses to the goodness in Christ.

In a situation like this, one will have to die, in order to bring life. In this sense, death will mean, quitting the job of conversion, and allowing the Holy Spirit to take it over completely. Once we can do that, we would be able to receive His blueprint for getting that individual saved. As we follow that blueprint we will be pleasantly surprised to discover that all that time we were angry, God was at work. He had never ceased to work on our side, even though we were not aware of it. Dying to a need like this, will end this kind of witnessing that is really no more than an organised harassment. Prayerfully we will be able to discover that God has a program for solving the problem. Once we are sure of that, then we start to cooperate with God no matter how long it takes. We will then witness only when He says we should, and limit the things we share to what He says we should share. All the anger, and all the struggle will then cease, and faith will be restored.

Parents that are fighting as it were for their childrens' salvation are quite often caught in this trap. They are so anxious about it that they almost become irrational, forgetting that they too took quite some time to make up their minds fully, and be totally committed to the Lord. When they die to their fears, then they will be able to release their children to God, confident that no matter what happens, *The Good Shepherd* will go to any length to ensure that the family stays together all through eternity. They will then concentrate in extracting that personal promise from Him in prayer, urging Him to allow them to see it all in their own life time.

The seed must die can prove quite a difficult concept to digest. Like the saying goes; "it is easier said than done". There is no doubt about the fact that it can be quite an up-hill task to get a pressing issue out of the way. There is even the basic conflict of whether such an approach is still faith. Sometimes it is convenient to rationalize that dying to free ourselves from the oppressive hold of a need amounts to unbelief.

But we must come to terms with the fact that so long as faith so called, has become nothing but worry, then it cannot acquire the spiritual momentum needed to effect the desired miracle.

I came across a comic poster the other day which says it all; "Worry ", it says, "is like a rocking chair. It gives you something to do, but it gets you nowhere." It is precisely because these situations are laden with worry, that one must die to them in order to give faith a fallow ground on which to thrive.

Again, there is a thought that is quite helpful when it comes to these hard pressing issues and the circumstances that surround them. This thought became crystallized in my mind at a recent teaching session as the Holy Spirit of God ministered to me.

It has to do with the fact that God's dealings with us can only be best understood in the context of eternity rather than time. For example, when the Bible says in Romans 8:28, *"And we know that all things work together for good to those who love God, to those who are the called according to His purpose"*, there are circumstances that force us to wonder whether we really do understand what that passage is saying.

The word will bring healing to a hurting heart, but the mind may still be at a loss as to how to grapple with a difficult situation that hurts deeply. The answer lies in this truth: *We must see our lives from an eternal perspective.* Things that happen to us here on earth have import both in time and in eternity. Eternal considerations override temporal considerations normally.

Put in other words, we may say that it is only in the context of eternity that our lives in time attain their full meaning.

This truth has sufficient basis in the word of God for us to accept it. If eternity is so important that God's only begotten Son can incarnate and die the death of a criminal in order to make it possible for the progeny or descendants of Adam, then our place in eternity like His place in eternity must take precedence over our place in time. The cross was part of this plan of redemption, and so the cross and all that it entailed physically and spiritually had to be. The Bible did say as much in the 12th chapter of Hebrews, verses 2 and 3.

"Looking unto Jesus, the author and the finisher of our faith, Who for the joy that was set before Him endured the cross, despising the shame, and has sat down at the right hand of the throne of God. For consider Him who endured such hostility from sinners against Himself, lest you become weary and discouraged in your souls."

What this implies is that the gains of eternity inherent in the eternal life provided for us in Christ Jesus, must of necessity take precedence over the gains in time. To compromise eternity for time will amount to ignorance of the import of eternity, its place and purpose. Every benefit in time is therefore seen as a fringe benefit which accompanies sons and daughters of the kingdom. But the kingdom demands themselves must supersede the drive to obtain the fringe benefits. In fact the motivation or drive to obtain more of the fringe benefits must remain to further the gains in eternity. Eternity must not be sacrificed for temporal benefits.

This is why one can die to a need, rather than have that need build a wedge between us and the Lord.

Dying to a need does not in anyway imply that the need will not be met. No, not at all. In fact if anything, it opens a new gateway of power with the Lord as we say eloquently to Him that He, the Almighty God is first in our lives, and nothing should be allowed to come between us and Him, nothing at all.

The Psalmist was echoing this thought in Psalm 84, verse 10, where he said: *"For a day in Your courts is better than a thousand. I would rather be a doorkeeper (*waiter) *in the house of my God Than dwell in the tents of wickedness."*

For those who might go on to interpret that as meaning abandonment of the faith struggle, he went further to add in verse 11:

"For the Lord God is a sun and shield; The Lord will give grace and glory; *No good thing will He withhold from those who walk uprightly.*"

In spite of the fact that the psalmist was fully aware of the goodness of the Lord, nonetheless, he determined in his heart that even if it was not possible to obtain these goodies, he would rather stay as a waiter in the house of the Lord than compromise with evil.

The Apostle Paul asked Bishop Timothy to remind the people that gain is not synonymous with godliness, neither is godliness meant to be just a means of gain. [1st Timothy 6:5]

Because we are fully aware of this, we determine to jettison anything that is destroying our precious relationship with the Lord so that we can be free to belong to the Lord totally.

It bears repeating to say that this in no way implies loss. In fact it is the point that our Lord Jesus made in John chapter 12, verse 25, where He said: *"He who loves his life will lose it, and he who hates his life in this world will keep it for eternal life"*. Indeed, the seed must die in order to live again. This is as true in agriculture, as it is in matters of life, temporal or eternal.

It behoves us to seek the Holy Spirit's guidance in every situation we find ourselves. As the Chief Counsellor, He is the only One most qualified to tell us when it is time to let go, so that life can come through death.

Chapter 17

FAITH BEYOND THE GRAVE

There is yet this other dimension of faith which I have chosen to call, *faith beyond the grave*, because of the passage that inspired my meditation on it.

In the gospel of John chapter 11, verses 1 to 44, we read a most illuminating story that vividly illustrates this dimension of faith.

Mary and Martha, sisters to Lazarus, all very close friends of Jesus, sent an urgent message to Jesus that their brother was seriously ill, and needed our Lord's immediate attention. When Jesus got their cry for help, He checked up with His Father in Heaven, and declared to His disciples:

"This sickness is not unto death, but for the glory of God, that the son of God may be glorified through it." [John 11:4 NKJ]

The Bible went on to say that Jesus loved Mary, Martha and Lazarus, but despite that, He waited two extra days before setting out to answer their call. This is quite instructive about the ways of God. Since God had determined to give His Son glory through this, the programme with which He will accomplish it, must be left to Him alone to decide.

Mary and Martha were not that well informed on this subject. But it is in their separate encounters with Jesus on

His arrival that we draw our dimension of faith. Let us pick up the story from there.

> "Then Martha, as soon as she heard that Jesus was coming, went and met Him, but Mary was sitting in the house. Then Martha said to Jesus, Lord if you had been here, my brother would not have died. But even now I know that whatever You ask of God, God will give You.
>
> Jesus said to her, Your brother will rise again.
>
> Martha said to Him, I know that he will rise again in the resurrection at the last day.
>
> Jesus said to her, I am the resurrection and the life, He who believes in Me though he may die, he shall live. And whoever lives and believes in Me shall never die. Do you believe this?
>
> She said to Him, Yes, Lord, I believe that You are the Christ, the Son of God, who is to come into the world." [John 11:20-27 NKJ]

When Mary came to Jesus, she repeated the same statement, which tended to suggest that this is what they and their friends had been saying in their home before Jesus arrived. Said Mary in verse 32; *"Lord if you had been here, my brother would not have died."* There lies our dimension of faith, buried in the statement made by the two sisters to Jesus.

Faith beyond the grave may tend to connote something that is entirely in the future, when the hope of eternal life will be fulfilled for those who have surrendered their lives to Jesus. But this is a dimension of faith we require for the now and now, rather than for the by and by.

Mary and Martha said to Jesus; *"Lord, if you had been here, our brother would not have died."* In other words, as far as they were concerned, Jesus could still have helped no matter how bad Lazarus was, provided He had met him alive. In other words, they had put a limit to their faith. They had held on tenaciously, hoping as their brother gasped for breath, that Jesus would just walk in and rescue him from the clutches of death. But the moment Lazarus breathed his last as it were, all their faith died with him. There was some element of finality which death had imposed on the situation. *They did not have faith beyond the grave.*

When Jesus arrived, He took time to inform Martha in the dialogue quoted above, that what He could do when Lazarus was alive, He could still do even now that he was dead. Martha thought all that was in the future.

Faith beyond the grave means being able to trust the Lord beyond the boundaries of reason, and natural expectation because we are quite familiar with God's omnipotence. One can use several illustrations.

Take the case of a single lady close on forty years, who had waited for Mr. Right to come along all these years. Several pressures become recognisable in the ten years surrounding age forty, for various biological reasons. Because of these pressures, a lot of anxiety and disquiet set in causing untold frustrations.

These anxieties stem from the fact that she had judged her situation like Mary and Martha and came to the same type of conclusion that they came to. That conclusion runs somewhat like this: "Lord, you really don't have a lot of time to answer this prayer. Whatever you are doing has to happen before I am forty years. You seem to have forgotten my biological cycle, and the fact that nothing much is expected to happen after the age of forty."

In other words, we go to the Lord and say, "Lord, opportunity is passing us by. Please do hurry up."

The way Jesus responded to Mary and Martha's desperate call, suggests that he was fully aware of the limit they had placed on their faith. They had judged Christ to be only capable of healing the sick, but not of raising the dead. They placed a limit to the Lord's ability to answer prayer.

This type of limit serves to destroy all faith, once the limit we have set has been superseded.

Being able to hold on beyond our reasonable limits is a dimension of faith that quietens our soul and our spirit, and enables us to continue to trust the Lord no matter what is happening all around us.

It is this kind of faith beyond the grave, that gives birth to very unusual miracles that bring glory to the name of the Lord.

There are several examples of this kind of situation. A barren woman approaching menopause, faces the same type of pressures particularly if she has longed for a family of her own. A young, up and coming executive, whose mentor is retiring from the company at a time his own foothold has not been well established, feels the same kind of pressure. A young man courting a lady may do it so desperately that he ends up souring the whole relationship, and rather than generate affection, he ends up generating resentment. This is because his attitude reflects this desperation that says; it is this or I am finished. Young ladies also reflect this desperation, and as a result many compromise their faith in a bid to secure an engagement. They go ahead to lower their Christian standards of morality in order to please the young man in the hope that it will secure the engagement. There is also the businessman or woman who sees a particular venture as the golden opportunity that must be netted or else, the future will be bleak. He or she then proceeds to lower standards or bend the rules of business ethics. The concept of *faith beyond the grave*, frees us completely from all these pressures, and allows us to hear what the Lord is saying to us clearly. Once the element of desperation is removed, then faith can thrive again unhindered, and we are once more consumed by the omnipotence of God. We become fully persuaded again that God is able to as it were, make stones praise the Lord, where men refuse to do so. It is at such occasions that we are compelled to say to our soul like the Psalmist: *"Be still my soul."*

We must be able to recognize those situations that must be approached in this way. Having recognized them, we must then confront them with examples of God's omnipotence as revealed in His word and in our experiences. This restores our faith, and we are thus able to continue to hold on to the promise of God that no matter what happens, He will come to us with the answers to our prayers.

Faith beyond the grave teaches us to hope against hope, as was testified of the patriarch Abraham, the acclaimed father of faith. He was fully persuaded, the Bible declares in Romans chapter 4, that God had the capacity to fulfill whatsoever He had promised.

"Abraham believed and hoped, even when there was no reason for hoping, and so became the father of many nations...He was then almost one hundred years old; but his faith did not weaken when he thought of his body, which was already practically dead, or of the fact that Sarah could not have children. His faith did not leave him, and he did not doubt God's promise; his faith filled him with power, and he gave praise to God. He was absolutely sure that God

would be able to do what he had promised. That is why Abraham, through faith was accepted as righteous by God." [Romans 4:18-23 GNB]

Chapter 18

CONVERSATIONAL PRAYER

Conversational prayer is the vital link between the various dimensions of faith. When an individual is confronted with a situation in life, he may respond in one of several ways. If he is familiar with the various dimensions of faith, he may then wonder how best to tackle the situation.

He might simply try them out one after the other. If confession and expectation do not work, then he will try praise and a little bit of patience, or he will try to figure out how to die to the need in order to release his faith from emotional and psychological pressures. As time progresses, he may wonder whether the situation is not becoming like that of Abraham, calling for a dogged faith.

Each time he gets to the end of the list, he may then begin again, as if he is on a merry-go-round.

But when we have learnt to talk with God, and hear the Lord talk back to us, then we are in a position to follow Him step by step, as He leads us from goal to goal, or from objective to objective.[*See Pathway to Conversational Prayer Vantage Press NY]

Being able to hear the Lord clearly a good many times, if not all the time, is the only way out of each and every impasse.

The Psalmist gave us a vivid description of the confusion that can arise in the life of a believer under pressure in Psalm 73. Dr. Martin Lloyd D. Jones Queens Physician, of blessed memory, aptly described this psalm as an example of *Faith On Trial.*

The Psalmist outlined the pressures he suffered.

> "God is indeed good to Israel, to those who have pure hearts. But I had nearly lost confidence; my faith was almost gone because I was jealous of the proud when I saw that things go well for the wicked." [Psalm 73:1-3 GNB]

The Psalmist proceeded in verses 4 to 12 to outline the life of the wicked; their prosperity, their pride and arrogance, their blasphemy, and their authoritarian ways on earth. As he thought of all these, he then lapsed into self pity.

> "Is it for nothing, then, that I have kept myself pure and have not committed sin...
>
> I tried to think this problem through, but it was too difficult for me, *until I went into Your temple.* Then I understood what will happen to the wicked." [Psalm 73:13, 16, 17 GNB]

By the Psalmist's own admission, continuous rumination only led to more and more frustration. But then when he went into the temple of the Lord and talked the matter over with God, he gained the vital insight he needed to understand the end of the wicked. It was only after then that he was able to appreciate how stupid he was allowing all those thoughts to hold sway in his mind.

> "When my thoughts were bitter and my feelings were hurt, I was as stupid as an animal; I did not understand you." [Psalm 73:21-22 GNB]

Subsequently, he resolved to let the Almighty God guide and instruct him always.

> "Yet I always stay close to you, and you hold me by the hand. You guide me with your instruction and at the end you will receive me with honour." [Psalm 73:23-24 GNB]

Conversational prayer is indispensable to an effective Christian life. We must be able to talk things over with God, so that He can give us insight into the true position of our various life situations, and then instruct us specifically as to what we should do to resolve the various dilemmas of our lives.

If we are not able to talk things over with God, then we are left only with speculation. Can it be this, or that? Which dimension of faith is most appropriate here or there?

Being able to talk things over with God makes our lives easier for us. Each day, we are able to go with the Lord one step at a time, till we begin to experience victory in every area of our lives.

Chapter 19

THE DIMENSIONS OF FAITH

Some years ago, I was in a meeting where a preacher said that he has all his prayers answered and all his needs met. I did not believe him, even though I had no reason not to. I suppose why I did not believe him was because I just did not think that was possible judging from my own experience.

As I struggled with the challenges that confronted me in my own life, the revelation that crystallized into this book started to come to me from the Lord. The Lord started to teach me that it is indeed possible to have all one's prayers answered, and all one's needs met. *The secret lies in being able to blend dimensions of faith with conversational prayer.*

The apostle James captured the revelation where he said:

"Now listen to me, you that say, Today or tomorrow we will travel to a certain city, where we will stay a year and go into business and make a lot of money. You don't even know what your life tomorrow will be! You are like a puff of smoke, which appears for a moment and then disappears. What you should say is this: *if the Lord is willing, we will live and do this or that.*" [James 4:13-15 GNB]

During conversational prayer, an individual has the opportunity to discuss every need of his with the Lord. The Lord will then direct him on what things he needs to pray for, and the things he had better forget. He might have had a burden for a certain issue before he went in, like the Psalmist, to discuss the matter with the Lord. As the Lord sheds light on the issue, he gains understanding and insight, and so is able to judge the issue better. The Lord may then direct him on precisely what he should do, and how to approach the matter in prayer.

I have testimonies from people with respect to how conversational prayer helped lift a burden. A gentleman testified how the Lord instructed him to simply praise Him, and as he started to praise the Lord, faith grew in his heart and the anointing left the throne room of God to meet his need. One can multiply examples.

Conversational prayer is indispensable to the effective utilisation of the dimensions of faith. It is the Lord who can say: "Son, continue to believe and confess; or son, you know what, so long as you are so anxious about this thing, you cannot exercise faith in it. What you need to do is to die to this need, so that creative faith can sprout again in your heart." Or He may say, son, if you want to know what I really feel about this thing, then stop asking me for it because it is not in My will for your life. Sometimes He may simply counsel patience, letting us to know that it is not yet *'the fullness of time'*, for the issue in question. And when we are face to face with those situations that have naturally imposed time limits, or situations that are time limited in themselves, He may step in to urge us to hold on for an unusual miracle, helping us thereby to have "faith beyond the grave."

Indeed, dimensions of faith will be less useful without conversational prayer. What we will have will be simply trial and error, which has frustrations inherent in it.

The Psalmist declared in Psalm 37:

> "The steps of a good man are ordered by the Lord; and he delighteth in his way. *Though he fall, he shall not be utterly cast down: for the Lord upholdeth him with his hand.*"

It is conversational prayer that makes this possible, and these steps are directed to various dimensions of faith, which will enable the individual develop and sustain creative faith. This he does by providing a framework built on God's word with which the Holy Spirit of God can work in his life.

Dimensions of faith therefore serve to ensure that we approach God with the right attitude for every situation. It ensures that our faith is not a monolithic structure, but on the contrary it is multi-dimensional ensuring that we respond appropriately to each situation.

As dimensions of faith are built into the individual in the Holy Spirit's School of Faith, we come to realize that a book like this has no end theoretically, as new lessons add on newer dimensions. It has a limitless end because the Teacher Himself is unlimited in His depth and wisdom. When we look around us, we notice that there are people who reflect various depths of grasp of the dimensions outlined here. By the same token, we may also find others who reflect dimensions that are not outlined here, but which nonetheless shine forth the wisdom of God.

This is as it should be, for we are all students in this one school of faith from which no one really graduates, until he or she arrives at the shores of eternity.

THE END

'How do I get my faith to work for me all the time?'
This is the sort of question that crosses the mind now and again, particularly that of those who have decided to trust the Almighty God daily in every area of life.

In this book, Dimensions of Faith, Dr. Onuzo has laid a solid basis for Bible faith. He reveals a scholarly grasp of the subject that is quite refreshing to the intellectual mind. This singular attribute has converted this book into a very strong evangelistic tool, which can be used to reach the multitudes that are still wavering in the valley of decision.

The Dimensions of Faith themselves as here revealed, serve a varied menu that provide a dynamic faith shield for every dart of the enemy. They offer various strategies to the Christian in his battle of faith against the world and the devil.

This book is quite compelling. What Okey Onuzo shares here is deeply bible based, and quite authoritative. It looks at the subject of Bible Faith from an angle that is different from the usual. It imparts new insights to old concepts, and so refreshes the mind and the spirit, clearing away various obstacles to faith.

It certainly will educate, illuminate and encourage every pilgrim

Also by the author:

Pathway To Conversational Prayer

The Convert and the Counsellor

From Everlasting to Everlasting

Marriage is Honourable